AMERICA'S
NATIONAL PARKS

CONTRIBUTING WRITERS:
JOHN BOSLOUGH
JOHN GATTUSO

CONSULTANT:
RICHARD TOURANGEAU

PUBLICATIONS INTERNATIONAL, LTD.

John Boslough is a nature and science writer whose articles have appeared in such publications as *National Geographic* and *Smithsonian*. He is a former science editor for *U.S. News & World Report* and the author of *Earth: A Photographic Journey*.

John Gattuso is the project editor and principal writer of more than half a dozen travel books in the *Insight Guide* series covering the National Parks, Native American Indians, the Old West, and several American cities.

Richard "Dixie" Tourangeau works for the National Park Service and is based at the agency's North Atlantic regional office in Boston. He has toured 37 national parks and visited 180 park system units since 1973. His tour suggestions have helped hundreds of travelers.

Map Illustration: **Paul Pearson**

Those who contemplate the beauty of the earth find reserves of strength that will endure as long as life lasts.

Rachel Carson

CONTENTS

National Park Service
U.S. Department of the Interior

National Park System Map and Guide

National Park Service Regional Offices

Alaska Region
National Park Service
2525 Gambell Street
Anchorage, AK 99503-2892
907-271-2737

Mid-Atlantic Region
National Park Service
143 South Third Street
Philadelphia, PA 19106-2818
215-597-7018

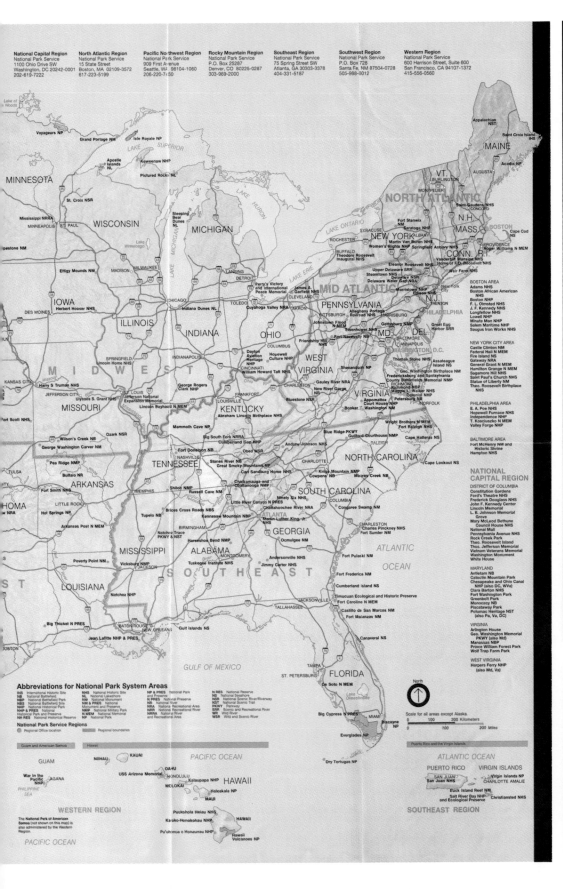

National Capital Region
National Park Service
1100 Ohio Drive SW
Washington, DC 20242-0001
202-619-7222

North Atlantic Region
National Park Service
15 State Street
Boston, MA 02109-3572
617-223-5199

Pacific Northwest Region
National Park Service
909 First Avenue
Seattle, WA 98104-1060
206-220-7450

Rocky Mountain Region
National Park Service
P.O. Box 25287
Denver, CO 80225-0287
303-969-2000

Southeast Region
National Park Service
75 Spring Street SW
Atlanta, GA 30303-3378
404-331-5187

Southwest Region
National Park Service
P.O. Box 728
Santa Fe, NM 87504-0728
505-988-6012

Western Region
National Park Service
600 Harrison Street, Suite 600
San Francisco, CA 94107-1372
415-556-0560

Abbreviations for National Park System Areas

IHS International Historic Site
NB National Battlefield
NBP National Battlefield Park
NBS National Battlefield Site
NHP National Historical Park
NHP & PRES National Historical Park and Preserve
NHS National Historic Site

NHS National Historic Site
NL National Lakeshore
NM National Monument
NM & PRES National Monument and Preserve
N MEM National Memorial
NMP National Military Park

NP National Park
NP & PRES National Park and Preserve
N PRES National Preserve
N RES National Reserve
NR National River
NRR National Recreational River
NRRA National River and Recreational Area

N RES National Reserve
NS National Seashore
NSR National Scenic River/Riverway
NST National Scenic Trail
PKWY Parkway
SRR Scenic and Recreational River
WR Wild River
WSR Wild and Scenic River

National Park Service Regions
⊙ Regional Office location
▬ Regional boundaries

NATIONAL CAPITAL REGION

DISTRICT OF COLUMBIA
Constitution Gardens
Ford's Theatre NHS
Frederick Douglass NHS
John F. Kennedy Center
Lincoln Memorial
L. B. Johnson Memorial Grove
Mary McLeod Bethune Council House NHS
National Mall
Pennsylvania Avenue NHS
Rock Creek Park
Theo. Roosevelt Island
Thos. Jefferson Memorial
Vietnam Veterans Memorial
Washington Monument
White House

MARYLAND
Antietam NB
Catoctin Mountain Park
Chesapeake and Ohio Canal NHP (also DC, WVa)
Clara Barton NHS
Fort Washington Park
Greenbelt Park
Monocacy NB
Piscataway Park
Potomac Heritage NST (also Pa, Va, DC)

VIRGINIA
Arlington House
Geo. Washington Memorial PKWY (also Md)
Manassas NBP
Prince William Forest Park
Wolf Trap Farm Park

WEST VIRGINIA
Harpers Ferry NHP (also Md, Va)

BOSTON AREA
Adams NHS
Boston African American NHS
Boston NHP
F. L. Olmsted NHS
J. F. Kennedy NHS
Longfellow NHS
Lowell NHP
Minute Man NHP
Salem Maritime NHS
Saugus Iron Works NHS

NEW YORK CITY AREA
Castle Clinton NM
Federal Hall N MEM
Fire Island NS
Gateway NRA
General Grant N MEM
Hamilton Grange N MEM
Sagamore Hill NHS
Saint Paul's Church NHS
Statue of Liberty NM
Theo. Roosevelt Birthplace NHS

PHILADELPHIA AREA
E. A. Poe NHS
Hopewell Furnace NHS
Independence NHP
T. Kosciuszko N MEM
Valley Forge NHP

BALTIMORE AREA
Fort McHenry NM and Historic Shrine
Hampton NHS

SANCTUARIES OF NATURE

Preserving the Wild for Future Generations

O ur national parks are as diverse and extraordinary as the land and people that make up our nation. With each passing year, as we better understand the impact we are having on our environment, we become more aware of the value of this important national resource.

The establishment of Yellowstone as the first national park in March of 1872 marked the beginning of a new attitude toward wilderness. Until that time, most Americans had thought of the nation's virgin forests, vast expanses of prairie, pristine waterways, incredibly rich mineral deposits, and other natural assets as sources of personal wealth to be used in whatever way any individual who owned them wanted. But the astonishing natural wonders of Yellowstone were a catalyst that began to change the prevailing American attitude about wilderness from a desire to exploit its treasures into a wish to protect them.

In the late 1860s, rumors began circulating in Washington. D.C., about an otherworldly land of bizarre topography, bubbling hot springs, geysers erupting a hundred feet in the air, and other phenomenal thermal spectacles in the Yellowstone region of the Rocky Mountains. Three men from Montana were dispatched to the area in 1869 to prove the rumors or put them to rest, but their reports left the public as skeptical as ever.

The following year, a survey team under the leadership of Henry Washburn, the Surveyor General of Montana, conducted a more thorough and systematic exploration of Yellowstone, ultimately concluding that even some of the most fantastic rumors about the place were true. Keeping careful records as they moved through the region, the 19 explorers named the thermal wonders, often picking epithets derived from the netherworld.

By law, the explorers were entitled to stake individual claims on the territory and its natural wonders. But one evening, at the junction of the Firehole, Gibbon, and Madison rivers, the men sat around what has proved to be one of history's most significant campfires. They had been talking about the way in which they were planning to divide Yellowstone among themselves, when one member of the expedition, a young attorney named Cornelius Hedges, eloquently proposed another alternative: Instead of seeking private gain, the men should persuade the federal government to preserve the Yellowstone region in its entirety.

All but one member of the party agreed. When the men returned home, they lobbied vigorously for government protection of the area. They were highly persuasive, and in March

Right: Stephen T. Mather, director of the National Park Service, leads an enthusiastic opening-day crowd through Yellowstone's Roosevelt Arch (north entrance) on June 20th, 1926.

of 1872, Congress passed legislation creating the world's first national park "as a pleasuring ground for the benefit and enjoyment of the people."

Of course, Cornelius Hedges doesn't deserve all the credit. He merely articulated a notion that had been circulating for years, although he and his companions were the first to see it to fruition.

The idea for a national park can be traced at least as far back as 1832, when a young painter named George Catlin, fearing that the western frontier would soon be overrun, proposed that the Great Plains be set aside as a "magnificent park."

"What a beautiful and thrilling specimen for America to preserve and hold up to the view of her refined citizens and the world in future ages!" he wrote. "A nation's park, containing man and beast, in all the wild[ness] and freshness of their nature's beauty."

Busy building a nation, however, most Americans weren't ready to hear what Catlin had to say. There were exceptions, those who, like Catlin, found a deeper value in nature. In the eastern United States, writers and thinkers like Ralph Waldo Emerson, Henry David Thoreau, and Walt Whitman looked to the natural world for spiritual renewal and a sense of the divine. Thoreau suggested that small parks be set aside in every town so that residents would never be far from the healing power of living things. "In wildness is the preservation of the world," he wrote, suggesting that experiencing nature is a deep human need.

In the West, the cause of wilderness was championed with greatest passion by John Muir, a self-taught naturalist and co-founder of the Sierra Club. Wandering the great mountain ranges of the West, particularly his beloved Sierra Nevada, Muir developed a vision of wilderness as an ecological and spiritual necessity.

Above: A painter who specialized in depicting scenes of Indian life—such as this 1832 painting, entitled "Big Bend on the Upper Missouri"—George Catlin was an early supporter of the conservation movement.

Top: Early this century, long before Minnesota had its first national park, vacationers were venturing into the state's wilderness areas to camp, hike, and canoe.

Bottom: An early mountain-climbing expedition breaks up camp before the long, dangerous trek to the top of Alaska's 20,320-foot Mount McKinley, the highest peak in North America, now the main feature of Denali National Park.

He sought union with the natural world as a living entity, climbing to the peak of a 100-foot fir in order to experience firsthand the rage of a windstorm, riding an avalanche above Yosemite Valley and calling it "the most spiritual and exhilarating of all the modes of motion," and hiking the Sierra for weeks at a time with little more than bread and tea to sustain him.

"Climb the mountains and get their good tidings," he advised his fellow Sierrans. "Nature's peace will flow into you as sunshine flows into trees. The winds will blow their own freshness into you and the storms their energy, while cares will drop off like autumn leaves."

A persuasive writer, Muir quickly became the voice of the conservation movement. He wielded his pen against loggers, sheepherders, and other "temple destoyers" who threatened his beloved Yosemite, and he campaigned for the creation of parks dedicated to mountains and forests elsewhere in the West.

"God has cared for these trees, saved them from drought, disease, avalanches and floods," Muir wrote, "but he cannot save them from fools. Only Uncle Sam can do that."

Slowly, perhaps even grudgingly, Uncle Sam acted. In 1890, after much campaigning and cajoling, Congress authorized Sequoia, General Grant (later incorporated into Kings Canyon), and Yosemite national parks in California. Several years later, Mount Rainier in Washington was added to the growing list.

Then, in 1901, Muir and his fellow conservationists found a powerful ally in President Theodore Roosevelt. An avid outdoorsman and a firm believer in the goals of the conservation movement, Roosevelt added more than 130 million acres to the national forests, launched a system of wildlife refuges, and created 18 national parks and monuments, including Petrified Forest, Mesa Verde, and Devils Tower.

"Leave it as it is," Roosevelt said of Arizona's Grand Canyon, which he saved from developers by designating it a national monument in 1908. "You cannot improve on it. Keep it for your children, your children's children, and for all who come after you as the one great sight which every American should see."

As Muir quickly learned, however, creating parks and protecting them were two very different things. In 1901, the city of San Francisco filed a request to dam the Tuolumne River in Yosemite National Park and drown the Hetch Hetchy Valley. Muir led a campaign against the project, but Congress was

Left: Theodore Roosevelt stands with conservationist John Muir atop Yosemite's Glacier Point in 1904. "Climb the mountains and get their good tidings," Muir advised all who would listen.

not persuaded. The dam was approved in 1913 and completed several years later.

The so-called rape of Hetch Hetchy was a major defeat for conservationists, but it galvanized supporters of the national parks. One of them, Stephen T. Mather, a wealthy Chicago entrepreneur, was invited by Secretary of the Interior Franklin Lane to take charge of park policy.

Mather advocated a centralized park administration, and in August of 1916, America's 35 national parks and monuments were placed under the supervision of the newly created National Park Service. Mather was appointed director and, together with his young assistant, Horace M. Albright, set about

shaping the mission of the National Park Service "to conserve the scenery and the natural and historic objects and the wild life therein and to provide for the enjoyment of the same in such manner and by such means as will leave them unimpaired for the enjoyment of future generations."

Mather and Albright immediately began to push for expansion. By the 1930s, a dozen natural areas and more than 40 historic sites were added to the National Park System, including large eastern reserves like the Great Smoky Mountains, Shenandoah, and the Everglades.

There was an important shift in philosophy, too. Parks weren't being set aside merely for their scenic beauty, but for

Right: Stephen Mather, far right, at a buffalo-steak dinner in honor of longtime colleague Horace M. Albright, far left. Mather was appointed the first director of the National Park Service in 1916. Albright later succeeded him as the agency's second director.

their ecological value as well. More than natural curiosities, they were seen as "vignettes of primitive America," pristine samples of New World ecology preserved in their original wild condition.

The proliferation of automobiles during the 1930s made national parks much more accessible to Americans, but most visitors were content to merely drive by the major sights for a quick look, preferring to be entertained by animal acts, drive-through sequoia trees, sound-and-light shows, and other amusements that were only marginally related to their wilderness setting.

By the 1950s, many Americans had gotten into the habit of making one national park the destination for an entire vacation. Family car campers routinely overfilled campgrounds, bringing with them all the comforts of home, including portable radios, charcoal cookers, and mountains of throwaway packaging material.

Beginning in the 1970s, the park service started to make difficult but necessary choices intended to return the parks to their original mandate. Use of the parks began to be limited to activities that are more in tune with the natural aspects of the parklands. As a result, natural cycles have been re-estab-

lishing themselves; food chains have been rebuilding. Animals that had almost completely disappeared, including buffalo, wolves, and white trumpeter swans, have been successfully reintroduced.

There is much that still needs to be accomplished, but it is comforting to know that the legacy of Catlin, Thoreau, Muir, and other early conservationists still guides the mission of the National Park Service. You can see it—indeed, feel it—every time you visit a national park.

One need only walk among the soaring sandstone cliffs of Zion National Park, the silent cliff-dwellings of Mesa Verde, the ancient forests of Great Smoky Mountains, the fractured granite cliffs of Acadia. It's an experience that people don't forget, and one that keeps them coming back with friends and family in order to share this precious gift. These are truly extraordinary places, the crown jewels of American wilderness, where the grandest landscapes and most diverse wildlife are protected by rangers, naturalists, and other members of the National Park Service.

With budgets growing ever tighter, the job isn't getting any easier. It's not that Americans don't care about the parks. In fact, if attendance is any indication (now totaling approximately 260 million annually), they may love them too much.

Top: The invention of the automobile made the parks more accessible to Americans—and started the popular tradition of drive-in camping.

Bottom: Recreational vehicles crowd a parking lot in the late 1970s. Of the many problems that beset the parks, overcrowding may be the most serious. Millions of people visit the parks every year, taxing services, facilities, and personnel.

13

Of the many problems that beset the parks, overcrowding may prove to be the most serious.

"We may love a place and still be dangerous to it," Wallace Stegner warned. "The best thing we have learned from nearly 500 years of contact with the American wilderness is restraint, the willingness to hold our hand, to visit such places for our souls' good, but leave no tracks."

These precious places are certainly worth protecting, because the national parks give us something that isn't easily found anywhere else—an understanding of ourselves in relation to nature, a sense of how vast and wondrous and varied the earth really is.

"The human spirit needs places where nature has not been rearranged by the hand of man," wrote William Breed. And that's exactly what the parks provide, places where we can remind ourselves that nature exists on its own terms, according to its own rules and rhythms. There's something genuinely comforting in that thought, something that touches our deepest feelings of awe and reverence for the magnificence of creation.

In an unfinished book, Rachel Carson calls this feeling simply "the sense of wonder," an almost childlike recognition that nature occupies a world "beyond the boundaries of human existence."

"Those who contemplate the beauty of the earth find reserves of strength that will endure as long as life lasts," she wrote. "There is symbolic as well as actual beauty in the migration of the birds, the ebb and flow of the tides, the folded bud ready for spring. There is something infinitely healing in the repeated refrains of nature—the assurance that dawn comes after night, and spring after the winter."

Perhaps this is the most telling statement about why we love the national parks. More than islands of nature, they are sanctuaries of the human heart. Now more than ever, the national parks deserve our support, our care, and, above all, our protection. Their future is in our hands.

Right: Wyoming's Snake River flows silently through Grand Teton National Park, providing rafters the opportunity to observe wildlife while enjoying the beautiful scenery.

ACADIA

Islands Primeval

Both dramatic and sublime, Acadia National Park is a nearly perfect summation of Maine's spectacular coast. Completely surrounded by the sea, the park's glacier-scoured interior consists of lovely valleys, lakes, and peaks. As they have for centuries, wave and wind sculpt its rugged coast.

Cadillac Mountain, which is 1,530 feet high, is one of the places where dawn first brushes the United States. Daylight greets this mountaintop, the highest point on the East coast between Canada's Gaspé Peninsula and Rio de Janeiro, in spectacular waves of purple, red, and blue. Four miles west, a deep coastal valley has been filled by the sea to create Somes Sound, the only true fjord in the contiguous 48 states. Across an inlet to the east, the Schoodic Peninsula is a remote, untamed intrusion into the ocean, where enormous granite rocks brace against the endless lashing of the waves.

The park is in a region that was once a French colonial territory called La Cadie. The area was first explored in 1604 by Samuel de Champlain. His ship crashed into a shoal off the coast and required extensive repairs. While Champlain's party was stranded, he led them ashore to explore the interior. There he encountered people from the Abnaki tribe who lived on the island during the summer. Because of its hills, moun-

tains, and rugged coast, they called it Pemetic, "the sloping land." Champlain renamed the pristine island, blessed with forests, lakes, and mountains, L'Isle des Monts Déserts, or "island of desert mountains," because from the sea it looked barren and wasted.

Interested mainly in the island's beavers because their pelts drew high prices in Europe, Champlain returned to France with wondrous tales. A French mission was established there a few years later. Following a century and a half of war between the French and British over control of the New World, the island finally fell into the hands of the English in 1763, just 13 years before the American Revolution.

During the late-nineteenth and early-twentieth centuries, a number of millionaires, includ-

Above: During the last ice age, a sheet of ice carried this boulder from a ledge at least 20 miles away to the top of Cadillac Mountain, the highest point on the East Coast.

Left: Rising to an elevation of 839 feet, the granite ramparts of Beech Mountain overlook Long Pond, gouged out of the earth by glaciers more than 10,000 years ago.

ACTION OF GLACIERS

Acadia National Park owes its dramatic beauty to the action of glaciers during one of the most recent ice ages.

Approximately two millennia ago, Mount Desert Island sat atop a steep granite ridge on the edge of the North American continental mainland. When enormous sheets of ice—some of them three miles thick—advanced from the north, glaciers flowed over the tops of the coastal mountains. When the great glaciers moved, they smoothed the tops of the mountains, scraping out large pits that later became lakes, at the same time gouging out valleys and passes through the mountains.

The glaciers began melting as the earth's atmosphere warmed. The corresponding rise in the level of the oceans flooded many of the coastal valleys, creating inlets and harbors and also cutting off sections of the shoreline from the mainland. A glance at the map makes it easy to see that Mount Desert Island was formed this way. Its lake-studded, mountainous interior is a testimony to the work of ice thousands of years ago.

ing John D. Rockefeller, began spending their summers on Mount Desert Island. By 1917, Rockefeller became convinced that the rapidly proliferating automobile would soon destroy the island's natural beauty and serenity, so he undertook the construction of an elaborate network of gravel paths. The roadways were for horse-drawn carriages only. Automobiles were not allowed on the 57 miles of paths and 17 granite bridges, each exquisitely built by hand. Later, Rockefeller donated the paths, bridges, and 11,000 acres of his own land to Acadia National Park.

Today, the park occupies about half the island, as well as several smaller islands. Private estates and charming coastal villages comprise the rest of Mount Desert Island. Rocke-

feller's carriageways are still in use and still not open to automobiles. Today they provide an easy, civilized, and inviting route into the park for walkers, horseback riders, bicyclists, joggers, and, in winter, cross-country skiers.

Left: Bass Harbor Head Light, built in 1858 to warn off passing ships, perches atop fractured granite cliffs at the southernmost point of Mount Desert Island.

Opposite: The soft light of morning breaks through sea fog to reveal fall's unmistakable colors alongside ancient rocks smoothed by glaciers.

19

ACADIA NATIONAL PARK

Established: 1919

Location: Maine

Size: 41,933 acres

When to go: Open all year (winter access is limited)

Terrain: Mountains, lakes, valleys, rugged coastline, and beaches

Highlights: Cadillac Mountain and Schoodic Peninsula

Wildlife: Muskrats, beavers, sea gulls, herring gulls, bald eagles, bullfrogs, bottle-nosed dolphins, small mammals, and birds

Activities: Ranger-led nature walks, films, slide shows, and bus tours; carriage rides, hayrides, hiking, cycling, horseback riding, swimming, fishing, cross-country skiing, snowshoeing, ice fishing, and snowmobiling

Services: Visitor center, museum, and two camp-grounds

Information: Acadia National Park, P.O. Box 177, Bar Harbor, Maine 04609; 207-288-3338

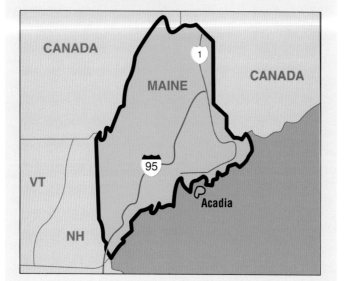

Right: The ocean pounds the East Coast relentlessly, wearing away everything but the earth's hard granite core.

AMERICAN SAMOA

Pacific Wonderland

Situated approximately 2,300 miles south of Honolulu, American Samoa National Park is closer to Auckland, New Zealand, than it is to any city in the United States.

Samoa is a dazzling chain of jewellike islands twinkling across a lonely expanse of the South Pacific. Five of the easternmost islands and two coral reefs comprise American Samoa National Park. Formed by volcanic activity originating on the floor of the ocean, the islands are a tropical paradise of mountains, rain forests, deep harbors, and stunning white beaches.

The national park preserves tropical rain forests, coral reefs, and an endangered 4,000-year-old culture. Tutuila, the largest island of American Samoa, is crowned with two great volcanic peaks rising above steaming rain forests. A great natural harbor nearly cuts the island in two. At its head lies fabled Pago Pago, sometimes called Pangopango, a South Seas island village that is American Samoa's capital and only port of call.

The northern and most accessible section of the park rises above Pago Pago's harbor in great volcanic ridges covered with dozen upon dozens of species of tropical trees and vegetation. The park encompasses coastal villages, tropical lagoons, and a dramatic scenic highway with fine views of a Pacific coral reef. Among the unusual wildlife found here are 35 species of brightly colored birds, as well as the endangered flying fox, which is actually a bat, but with the wingspan of an eagle.

The largest section of the park, about 5,000 acres, lies on Ta'u, the easternmost island and a half-hour flight from Pago

Pago. This section includes Lata Mountain, which seems to rise nearly straight up from the Pacific and at 3,170 feet is the highest volcano in the islands. The Ta'u section of the park also includes 300 offshore acres.

The park's smallest section is on Ofu, a volcanic island just west of Ta'u. It encompasses only 260 acres of land and water, but has one of the finest beaches in the South Pacific. Most people would agree that this stretch of white sand and stately palms defines what a tropical paradise should look like. Lying just offshore and protecting a lovely blue lagoon, a healthy coral reef teems with a vast array of sea life.

For more than 4,000 years, members of Polynesia's oldest culture have lived on these islands. Samoa means "sacred earth," the name reflecting the belief of the people that the islands are a special place to be cherished and protected. In 1988, believing that their own ancient culture also needed protection, Samoan chiefs agreed to lease some of their ter-

Above: Across Afono Bay, Polo Island juts out of the ocean. The worn volcanic peak will eventuallly succumb to the erosive action of wind and wave.

Opposite: The view from Mount Alava reveals the intense blue of South Pacific waters framed by the lush green of a dense coastal forest.

ritory to create a national park. Permanent leasing arrangements are still being worked out, and visitors must obtain permission to enter this new and unusual park.

AMERICAN SAMOA NATIONAL PARK

Established: 1988

Location: American Samoa

When to go: Open all year, but permission is required to enter

Size: 9,000 acres (approximately 1,000 acres underwater)

Terrain: Volcanic islands, tropical rain forests, beaches, and coral reefs

Highlights: Lata Mountain, rain forests, and coral reefs

Wildlife: Flying foxes and 35 tropical bird species

Activities: Tours, swimming, and walking

Services: All visitor facilities are currently located outside the park.

Information: American Samoan Office of Tourism, P.O. Box 1147, Pago Pago, American Samoa 96799; 011-684-633-1091 (92/93)

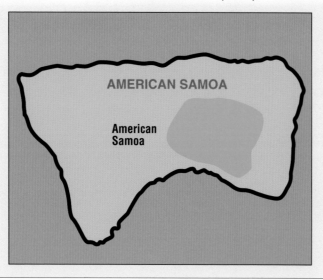

Top Right: The beaches on the island of Ofu are spectacularly beautiful. Offshore, a vibrant coral reef shelters large numbers of brightly colored tropical fish.

Opposite: The azure waters and brilliant white beaches of remote Ofu Island are fringed by lush tropical vegetation clinging to the slopes of steep volcanic mountains.

FORMATION OF A CORAL REEF

Visitors to American Samoa National Park have an opportunity to see firsthand some of the best preserved coral reefs in the Pacific Ocean.

The reefs harbor an astonishing array of sea life. Vibrantly colored fish in hundreds of varieties dart around the spectacular limestone formations that protect them from the vagaries of the weather, strong Pacific currents, and such predators as the several species of sharks that haunt the reefs.

Coral reefs are produced over centuries by the secretions of colonies of tiny polyps, usually stony corals. The accumulation of their skeletal material is gradually broken and piled up by the motion of the waves. The structure of the reefs changes constantly, although this is not evident to the casual observer.

There are three kinds of coral reefs: the barrier reef, which usually lies far offshore and protects a wide deep lagoon, such as Australia's Great Barrier Reef; the atoll, a reef surrounding a lagoon with no central island; and the fringing reef, a coral platform close to the shore that follows the coastline, such as the reef found in American Samoa National Park.

ARCHES

Windows on the Desert

Chiseled by the powerful forces of wind and water, this surprising natural rock garden contains the planet's most remarkable collections of abstract sculpture. Arches National Park sits on a great plateau in southeastern Utah, encompassing a stark landscape of broken red sandstone. The park contains more than 2,000 natural stone arches. But these spectacular sandstone portals, braced against the desert sky and revealing lovely desert terrain through their openings, are only part of Arches' stunning landscape.

A fantasyland of rock, the park is filled with giant balanced rocks that look as though they are about to teeter and fall. There are pedestals and spires that resemble a child's drip castles enlarged to enormous scale. Glistening slickrock domes are inlaid with swirls of stone cut by red sandy washes and dotted with wildflowers in spring. These formations sparkle and shimmer beneath an enormous blue sky.

Arches is perched atop the Colorado Plateau, a high desert region stretching from western Colorado across southern Utah and northern New Mexico to Arizona. This area is the most sparsely populated region of the contiguous 48 states, but it contains the nation's greatest wealth of national parks. It is a place teeming with scenic treasures almost beyond belief: mountains, gorges, rushing rivers, great canyons, escarpments, buttes, spires, pinnacles, and endless stretches of desert landscape.

High above the Colorado River, Arches National Park is a geological maelstrom that has been shaped by eon after eon of weathering by rain, snow, ice, and wind. Most of the formations in the park are composed of Entrada sandstone,

which geologists say was part of a low arid coastal plain adjacent to a great inland sea 150 to 200 million years ago. Over time, the sand was covered by layers of sediment and hardened into rock. Then the land was lifted up, tilted, and eroded until the Entrada layer was exposed to the weather. At first, water and wind cracked the exposed sandstone. Then, narrow canyons and gullies were scoured out of the stone, leaving thin walls called "fins" in between.

Left: Balanced Rock looks precarious, but geologists estimate that it has taken nature 60 million years to create this masterpiece and expect it will take millions more years to erode the spire and topple the rock.

Opposite: The sheer walls of The Organ, one of several sandstone monoliths in an area known as Park Avenue, are reflected in water-filled potholes, an important source of moisture in this otherwise arid environment.

The next phase in the process occurred as wind and frost brushed away at the soft interior area of some of these fins, eventually perforating them with a window. Such an opening gradually enlarged until the window became an arch. The park's most photographed attraction, Delicate Arch, is isolated in its own amphitheater, framing a stunning view of endless sandstone. Landscape Arch, with a span of 306 feet, is the longest in the world and only one of seven arches along the two-mile-long Devils Garden Trail.

Top Right: Landscape Arch defies the laws of engineering. It is 291 feet long, 65 feet high, and only six feet thick at its narrowest point—and getting thinner.

Right: Delicate Arch, which is 65 feet tall and 35 feet wide, perches on the rim of a canyon. The arch is all that remains of a huge sandstone wall called a fin.

ARCHES SCENIC DRIVE

Arches National Park is more than a concentration of spectacular rock arches. Well-preserved petroglyphs carved into a cliff in the park testify that people have inhabited the region for a long time. The pictures depict riders on horseback, indicating that the carvings were made sometime after the middle of the sixteenth century when Spanish explorers first introduced horses to the Southwest.

These petroglyphs increase our sense of the timelessness of this place. We know that the landscape here is constantly changing. Such natural spectacles as the Fiery Furnace, a dense array of red fins, could one day become arches. But today we admire them as they appear to turn into tongues of fire when the sun is low in the sky.

The scenic drive through Arches climbs from the floor of Moab Canyon to Devils Garden. Along this 18-mile, one-way drive you pass a lovely slickrock expanse called the Petrified Dunes. With the snowcapped La Sal Mountains rising in the distance, the dunes are a spectacle of form and contrast.

Other sights are equally spectacular: Balanced Rock, a striking, eroded stone spire 128 feet high; South Window Arch, 105 feet wide; and the dramatic Double Arch.

ARCHES NATIONAL PARK

Established: 1971

Location: Utah

When to go: Open all year (the best seasons are spring and fall)

Size: 77,739 acres

Terrain: High desert plateau with unusual rock formations

Highlights: Delicate Arch and Fiery Furnace

Wildlife: Small desert mammals, reptiles, and birds

Activities: Ranger-led walks and evening programs; self-guided auto tour, hiking, float and powerboat trips, jeep tours, horseback riding, and backpacking

Services: Visitor center and one campground

Information: Arches National Park,
P.O. Box 907,
Moab, Utah 84532;
801-259-8161

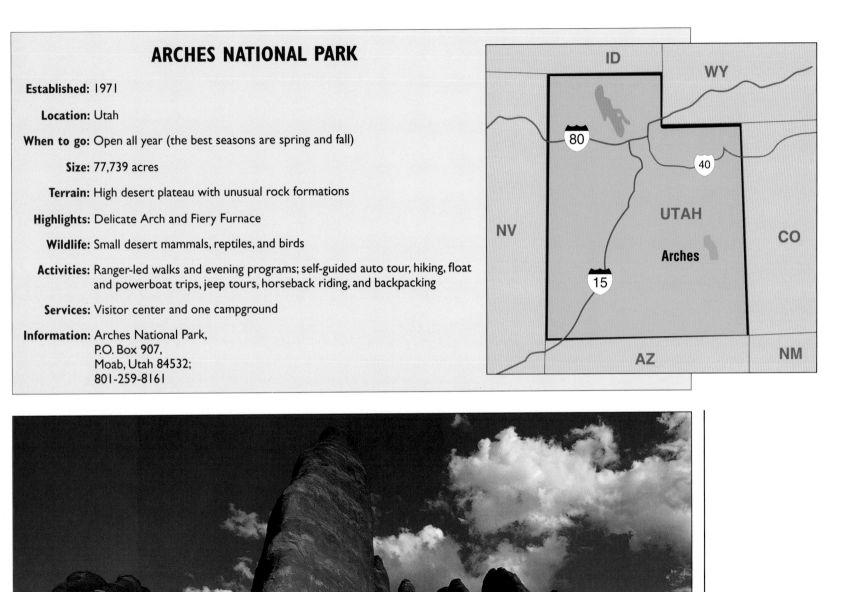

Left: The Fiery Furnace in Arches is a labyrinth of salmon-colored Entrada sandstone fins. The snow-capped La Sal Mountains are about 20 miles southeast of the park.

BADLANDS

Fantasyland

This stunning amalgamation of rock spires, castles, cathedrals, and battlements—almost 100 miles long and 50 miles wide—cuts across the Great Plains of southwestern South Dakota. But you can walk or drive across the rolling grasslands almost to its borders without being aware that this vast expanse of other-worldly terrain is nearby.

Suddenly, in a matter of a few yards, you are amid a theatrical and bewildering jumble of towers and imposing buttresses. Rock palaces, hundreds of feet high, loom large against big prairie sky. The terrain of the area is so arid and the land formations so eerie that the Sioux called this place *mako sica*, or "bad land." French-Canadian trappers called it *les mauvaises terres à traverser*, or "bad lands to cross."

Early pioneers avoided the Badlands, but people have lived among these strange formations for millennia. Within Badlands National Park, more than 80 archeological sites have been discovered, indicating that the first humans arrived in the area as long as 7,000 years ago. These people were probably nomadic hunters and gatherers who may have been among the early arrivals from Asia across the Bering land bridge.

In more recent times, the Dakota Indians, more commonly known as the Sioux, were masters of the northern plains. During the last

years of their wars with the United States, they used the remote Badlands as their stronghold against the U.S. Army.

In the late 1880s, the Sioux adopted a mystical religious movement that incorporated what became know as the Ghost Dance. Other Indian tribes, such as the once-feared Comanche, who were making a last stand against encroaching white settlers on the southern plains, also embraced these beliefs. The Ghost Dance cere-

Left: More than 60 million bison once roamed North America. Today, scattered herds are protected in national parks and other reserves. Some animals, like this shaggy bull, may weigh a ton or more.

Far Left: Bands of soft color recall the long history of a plain that was eroded by the powerful forces of wind and water.

31

BADLANDS GEOLOGY

Badlands are found in many parts of the world. This kind of geological formation usually occurs in semi-arid climates and is characterized by countless gullies and ridges, as well as sparse vegetation.

The term "badlands" was first used to describe the area of South Dakota that is the world's most extensive and best example of this kind of topography. The Badlands are cut from deep alluvial and volcanic ash deposits that have been sculptured and carved into fantastic forms by the continuous action of wind and water falling in infrequent but torrential downpours.

It all began about 80 million years ago when the Pierre shale, the bottom layer of the Badlands geology, was laid down by a great inland sea. About 35 million years ago, rivers and streams running downhill from the Black Hills spread sand, mud, and gravel on the area. Volcanic activity, probably originating in the Rocky Mountains to the west, poured vast quantities of wind-borne ash on the plains of South Dakota.

For a few more million years, the land built up faster than it was eroded away. Then the balance changed, and wind and water went to work to create the geological wonderland we see today.

mony, which could take days to perform, promised that the white farmers and ranchers would disappear and that the buffalo would return.

The ritual was outlawed by the U.S. government, but for many years the Sioux danced without interference in the Badlands. The last Ghost Dance took place in 1890 on Stronghold Table just a few days before more than 150 followers of Big Foot, chief of the Miniconjou Sioux, were massacred by U.S. troops at Wounded Knee, 25 miles to the south. Today, Stronghold Table is at the end of a long rutted road that winds through lonely grassland. It is a haunting place that seems to

Left: Rain turns the Wall into a gooey mess of gray clay so slippery that it often cannot support its own weight, causing pieces of the cliffs to slide off.

Badlands: Fantasyland

be alive with the memories of this last dance before the final defeat and capitulation.

Despite the unfavorable reputation of the Badlands in the nineteenth century, at least one early visitor was fascinated by this stark and angry landscape eroded out of the surface of the prairie. In 1848, Fray Pierre-Jean DeSmet wrote: "Viewed at a distance, these lands exhibit the appearance of extensive villages and ancient castles." People visiting the park today are likely to get the same impression, especially when they look at the park's most monumental geological formation, the Wall.

Dividing the northern grasslands from those in the south, which are about 200 feet lower in elevation, the great Badlands Wall extends for 100 miles. This multitude of pinnacles, spires, pillars, shelves, and chimneys is an immense natural barrier cutting through the landscape. The Wall is almost impossible to see from the northern plains, but it rises above the southern plains like an ancient and abandoned city skyline.

In the Badlands, water is the force that sculpts the earth, but this powerful element is assisted by winds that "sandblast" the stone with airborne grit and dust. An annual cycle of freeze and thaw also contributes to the ongoing creation of the Wall, which is occurring at a phenomenal rate, geologically speaking. Photographs taken just 50 years ago show different formations than those seen today; this is the result of unusually rapid erosion. Measurements by geologists confirm that the Wall's surface is wearing away at an almost unbelievably fast pace; in some places, an inch or more is removed from the surface each year.

Today, with the Sioux defeated and the pioneers long gone, the Wall is the picturesque backdrop for a herd of buffalo. The animals were reintroduced into the area in 1963 after having been nearly exterminated by white hunters in the nineteenth century. Also wandering on the endless grasslands are lovely and graceful pronghorn antelope. Rocky Mountain bighorn sheep were brought to Badlands in 1964, and coy-

Right: A winter sunset washes the otherworldly landscape of the Badlands with a warm pink glow that contours the harsh terrain.

34

Top: Like all coyotes, those found in the Badlands prefer a diet of rodents and rabbits, but they also feed on carrion and a variety of plants.

Center: Weighing as much as 250 pounds or more, mountain lions (also known as cougars or pumas) are the largest predators in the park. Though rarely seen, their screamlike roar is unmistakable.

Bottom: The pronghorn is usually seen in small herds grazing on prairie grass and leafy plants. It is an extremely swift animal, able to sprint across the prairie at 45 miles per hour over short distances.

otes roam throughout the park as well. Other animals that once lived here—the grizzly bear, gray wolf, and American elk—are gone.

Gone for an even longer time are such creatures as the titanothere, an early ancestor of the horse that was about 12 feet tall and fed on prairie grasses millions of years ago. Some of the world's richest fossil beds are located in the Badlands. The remains of hundreds of prehistoric animals have been found, including an ancestor of the camel; a sheeplike creature with three horns, called the protoceras; and the fierce saber-toothed tiger.

The Badlands is a unique region, rich in history and geology. Someone once said: "It's a good place that's gotten a bad name." Anyone who appreciates a surprising and unusual land of rare natural beauty will agree.

HIKING THE WALL

The Windows Overlook is the trailhead for three nature walks, each of which gives visitors an excellent look at a unique piece of Badlands' geology by leading them into different sections of the Wall.

The Door Trail takes you just a few steps through a notch in the wall and onto what seems like the surface of the moon: a tangle of wildly eroded and barren hills that is the heart of Badlands.

Even more spectacular, the Notch Trail winds up the Wall to a window, or notch, eroded out of the top of a cliff. It faces southwest toward Cliff Shelf and Cedar Pass. At one point on the trail, you must climb straight up a wooden ladder on the face of a claystone cliff. The view is wonderful: prairie and badlands, the White River, and in the distance, the Pine Ridge Indian Reservation.

Almost equally beautiful, the Windows Trail leads to a spectacular natural window in the Wall that overlooks an unexpectedly deep canyon cut into the tableland.

Left: Erosion exposes layered sediment deposited millions of years ago by an ancient sea. The oxidation of iron, manganese, and other minerals creates vivid colors.

BADLANDS NATIONAL PARK

Established: 1978

Location: South Dakota

When to go: Open all year

Size: 243,244 acres

Terrain: Badlands and prairie

Highlights: The Wall

Wildlife: Buffalo, pronghorn antelope, mule deer, coyotes, prairie dogs, Rocky Mountain bighorn sheep, and prairie rattlesnakes

Activities: Ranger-led nature walks and fossil demonstrations, hiking, and backpacking

Services: Two visitor centers, two campgrounds, and a park lodge

Information: Badlands National Park,
P.O. Box 6, Interior,
South Dakota 57750;
605-433-5361

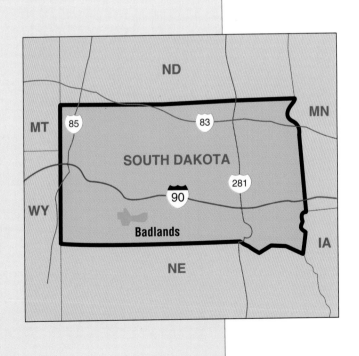

BIG BEND

Rio Grande Country

Sixteenth-century Spanish explorers traipsed through the valley of the Rio Grande in what is now southern Texas.

According to legend, they discovered a rich lode of silver at the top of a jagged mountain near a bend in the river where it had cut a spectacularly deep canyon. The Spanish soldiers enslaved the native people to work the mine, but eventually the miners rebelled, killed their Spanish overlords, and sealed the entrance to the mine so they would never have to work there again.

Looking like an abandoned castle atop a hill, Lost Mine Peak today is a landmark of Big Bend National Park, which encompasses an immense expanse of dry mountains, canyons, and desert wilderness just across the Rio Grande from Mexico.

Here the river winds south, then suddenly veers north in a great horseshoe curve before turning southward again. The region within the great triangle—an area as large as Massachusetts and Connecticut combined—is known as Big Bend country.

Forming the southern border of the park, the Rio Grande has sliced a deep chasm, called Santa Elena Canyon, through red and orange rock. The canyon is so deep and narrow in places that the sun barely penetrates it.

This is a wild land with a wild history. People arrived in Big Bend country about 10,000 years ago. They were probably nomadic tribes whose ancestors had recently crossed the Bering land bridge from Asia. The first farmers began cultivating the rich bottomland near the river in the thirteenth century A.D. These people may have wandered into the valley from Pueblo cities to the north.

When Spanish soldiers and settlers arrived in the sixteenth century, they captured the indigenous people and sold them as slaves. Soon, more warlike tribes, such as the Mescalero Apaches, moved in from the north, launching lightning attacks on the Spanish settlements.

Later the Comanches made their way into the region, driven by encroaching white settlers

Above: The Rio Grande flows along the park boundary for 118 miles; an additional 127 miles are protected by the Park Service. Popular with river runners, it features long stretches of calm water punctuated by spine-tingling rapids.

Opposite: A bouquet of creamy yellow blossoms crowns a patch of prickly pear cactus in the Chisos Mountains.

from the Comancheria, their prairie homeland in northwest Texas. Skilled horse fighters, the Comanche warriors victimized both Spanish ranchers and Apaches, killing, taking slaves to sell in Mexico, and destroying livestock and crops. They eventually drove the Spanish settlers from the region. In 1821, Big Bend country became part of Mexico and, 15 years later, part of the Republic of Texas.

Hundreds of millions of years ago, first one and then another great inland sea flowed through the region, depositing thick layers of limestone and fossil-bearing shale. About 60 million years ago, mountains began thrusting up through the earth. At about the same time, a 40-mile-wide plain began sinking along fault lines. This left the awesome cliffs of Santa Elena Canyon to the west and the Sierra del Carmen mountains to the east.

Then, about 35 million years ago, volcanic activity began spewing vast amounts of ash and dust into the air and squeezing out magma, or molten rock, to form the Chisos Mountains. Some of the magma that cooled and hardened underground was later exposed by erosion.

Today, Big Bend remains a special place; it is at once desolate, haunting, and fascinating. Within the park are archaeological treasures, petrified trees, vestiges of prehistoric cultures, and unusual forms of plant and animal life. Geologically, the park encompasses some of the most fascinating and complex landforms on earth.

Below: The Rio Grande flows through the desert, bringing life to a parched landscape. The ribbonlike oasis allows a wide variety of wildlife to survive in an otherwise extremely hostile environment.

EXPLORING BIG BEND

The Chisos are mountains of legend. Look closely at Pulliam Bluff in Chisos Basin, and you might see the profile of a reclining man's face. According to legend, this is Alsate, a mighty Apache chief whose ghost still roams the higher mountains. His campfire can still be seen at night, it is said.

The mountains are ideal for hiking, and many of the choicest outings begin from the trailhead in Chisos Basin. One of these, a short stroll up Window View Trail, reveals a photogenic formation called the Window, a deep V-shaped opening through which water drains from the basin. This spot is especially lovely at sunset, when vivid colors streak the sky and long shadows add mystery to the landforms.

Visitors can also walk to the Window for a spectacular view of a mountain called Casa Grande, or "Big House." Dawn and dusk add to the spectacle of this especially stunning vista. On the South Rim, you will find a fine oasis of bigtooth maple, Douglas fir, and Arizona pine. This is the yellow Colima warbler's only home in the United States.

Above: A "window" of precariously balanced rocks awaits hikers at the end of a moderate, two-mile trail into the Grapevine Hills, offering some of the loveliest desert scenery in the park.

Left: Winter seems out of place in a desert park like Big Bend, but January usually dusts the Chisos Mountains with light snow.

Above: The 1,500-foot limestone cliffs of Santa Elena Canyon hold the mighty Rio Grande to a narrow channel and allow sunlight to penetrate the depths only briefly each morning.

Opposite: The Chihuahuan Desert is subject to extreme weather. Summer temperatures routinely exceed 100 degrees, and snow occasionally falls in winter, especially in the higher elevations.

BIG BEND NATIONAL PARK

Established: 1944

Location: Texas

When to go: Open all year (fall and winter are the best seasons)

Size: 802,541 acres

Terrain: Canyons, mountains, river, and desert

Highlights: The Window and Casa Grande

Wildlife: Deer, mountain lions, javelinas, and hundreds of bird species

Activities: Ranger-led nature walks, raft trips, and evening programs; hiking, fishing, river rafting, horseback riding, bird-watching, nature seminars, and backpacking

Services: Two visitor centers, information stations, park lodge, four campgrounds, and a trailer park

Information: Big Bend National Park, Texas 79834; 915-477-2251

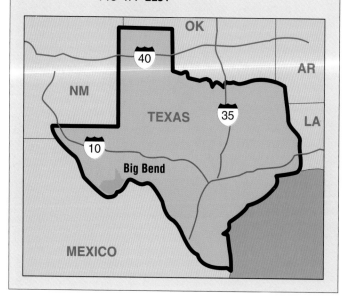

LIFE IN BIG BEND

The remarkable topographic variety within Big Bend provides a habitat for a surprising diversity of life. Here are 1,000 plant species, many found nowhere else on earth, and more than 400 species of birds, which is many more than you will find in any other national park.

Desert vegetation covers most of the park's terrain; bunchgrasses, cactus, creosote bushes, and yuccas grow in vast profusion. Also abundant are sotols, bright green plants with sawtooth edges on their leaves that the Apaches roasted and ate. Fermenting the plant yields an alcoholic drink.

A heavy spring rain can momentarily transform the desert. Normally dry creek beds rage with water, and dormant seeds create short-lived fields of wildflowers. Elsewhere in the park, the Rio Grande, with its deep canyons and floodplains, creates an ecosystem all its own, as do the cool Chisos Mountains, which harbor forests of pine and oak that provide a habitat for deer, mountain lions, and other animals.

BISCAYNE

Living Coral

Warmed by Gulf Stream waters flowing up through the sea like an immense river, Biscayne Bay extends eastward from the heavy mangrove forests of southern Florida to a string of low-lying barrier islands and coral reefs that protect it from the ocean.

During the seventeenth century, this bay was the hideaway of the notorious pirate Black Caesar. He lured his prey with a tricky ruse of pretending to be adrift in an open boat. When passing ships stopped to rescue the pirate, his crew fell upon them in ambush.

The pirates are now long gone; today, Biscayne Bay is patrolled by manatees. With their gentle, doleful faces, these enormous mammals can grow as long as 13 feet and weigh a ton or more. Manatees use their front flippers to shove sea grasses and other underwater plants into their mouths. There are only about 1,000 of these great beasts left; all of them roam the waters of Florida.

The bay also contains a remarkably varied spectrum of fish, fantastically shaped coral, and vast beds of waving turtle grass. The bay is only four to 10 feet deep, making it a breeding ground for more than 200 kinds of marine creatures, including shrimp, spiny lobsters, sponges, and crabs. Looking into the shallow water, you might be able to see the colorful flash of a parrot fish swimming by, the bright glimmer of an angelfish, or the surprisingly graceful movements of an immense sea turtle.

The park encompasses Biscayne Bay between Key Biscayne and Key Largo, the northernmost islands of the Florida keys. It is the only national park that is almost entirely underwa-

ter. Only four percent of its area is on dry land; the rest is an ocean wonderland.

The surface areas of the park consist of about 50 barrier islands strung across the water like pearls on a string and the magnificent mangrove shoreline that is the one the East Coast's major undeveloped coastal areas. The mangroves help stabilize this shoreline by trapping their own fallen leaves in networks of tangled roots. This decaying matter, rich in protein, provides food for the tiny creatures that occupy the bottom of the bay's extensive food chain. The mangroves also attract many species of birds, including peregrine falcons and bald eagles.

Like nearby Everglades National Park, Biscayne Bay was created by Congress under intense pressure from environmentalists, sportsmen, and other concerned citizens who wanted to save the bay from the threat of developers. In the 1960s, plans were made to build resorts and subdivisions on

Above: A great blue heron and snow-white great egret perch atop a mangrove. The birds are patient hunters, remaining perfectly still until they can spear a fish or frog on their sharp bills.

Opposite: The shallow waters of Biscayne Bay pose a severe threat to unwary ships. Cape Florida Lighthouse on Key Biscayne marks the northern boundary of the bay.

Top: Wading birds, such as this flock of beautifully colored roseate spoonbills, congregate at ponds, estuaries, and other wetland areas to feed on a bounty of shrimp and small fish.

Center: Red mangrove forests have made the islands of Biscayne National Park natural bird sanctuaries. The dense and tangled root systems of the mangroves keep out predators that cannot fly.

Bottom: Fiddler crabs scour mud flats for a morsel of food washed ashore by the receding tide. Male fiddlers use their one oversized claw in displays of aggression with other crabs.

the northern keys and to put an oil refinery on the adjacent mainland. To prevent this from happening, Biscayne Bay was made a national monument in 1968. The protected area was expanded to its present size, which encompasses more keys and reefs, when it became a national park in 1980. Today, the park covers more than 170,000 acres.

CORAL REEF

The most prominent life-forms in Biscayne National Park are the extensive communities of underwater coral reefs. These are the only living reefs within the continental United States.

Coral comes in many forms. As park visitors tour the bay in glass-bottom boats, the floorshow includes giant brain coral and mountainous star coral. Some of these coral reefs are extremely tall, rising hundreds of feet from the seafloor, with branching shapes that reach out in every direction.

Coral reefs are formed over centuries as colonies of tiny polyps secrete an exoskeleton of calcium carbonate, or limestone, then live within the tiny nooks and crannies of the ever-growing formation. The accumulation of this skeletal material, broken and piled up by wave action, eventually produces a huge, rocky mass that can support an astonishing variety of animal and plant life.

All the reefs of Biscayne Bay harbor an array of vibrantly colored fish that flit and flow around the gorgeous formations. You will see filefish, porcupine fish, angelfish, and sharks. Not all coral is hard as rock. In Biscayne Bay, you will also see soft corals, such as sea fans, rippling in the calm, clear water.

Left: Red mangroves stand on a tangle of proplike roots in shallow water off Elliott Key, creating a protected environment for juvenile shrimp, lobsters and a variety of fish.

BISCAYNE NATIONAL PARK

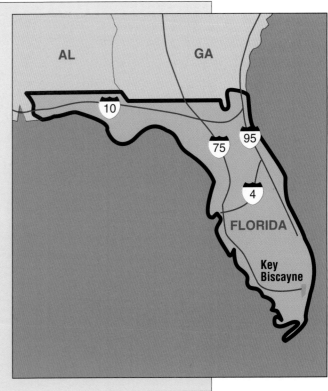

Established: 1980

Location: Florida

When to go: Open all year

Size: 173,039 acres

Terrain: Underwater coral reefs, barrier islands, and coastal areas

Highlight: Star coral reef

Wildlife: Pelicans, coral, manatees, sea turtles, sharks, eagles, and many species of tropical birds and fish

Activities: Ranger-led canoe trips, natural tours, and glass-bottom boat trips; swimming, snorkeling, scuba diving, water-skiing, boating, fishing, hiking, bird-watching, and backcountry camping

Services: Visitor center, two information stations, and two boat-in campgrounds

Information: Biscayne National Park,
P.O. Box 1369,
Homestead, Florida 33090;
305-247-7275

BRYCE CANYON

Palaces in Wonderland

The landscape is totally outlandish at Bryce Canyon. This is a place that looks like it has been gouged out of the earth, then filled with orange and red rock pedestals so fancifully and bizarrely formed that they look like the inhabitants of a dreamworld.

Endless rock towers called hoodoos take on all kinds of shapes, resembling castles, bridges, towers, presidents, prime ministers, and even Queen Victoria. The questionable practice of affixing names to geological formations is forgivable here.

Bryce Canyon is the scalloped edge of a huge mesa and not a true canyon. It is a series of great amphitheaters eroded out of the Paunsaugunt Plateau in southwestern Utah. On a grand scale, the geological formation containing Bryce resembles a loaf of bread that has been chewed away on one side. Erosion has taken about a dozen big bites out of the pink cliffs that form the plateau's eastern rim.

The Bryce escarpment, with its thousands of geological gargoyles and castellated spires, is the product of the relentless destructive powers of water and time. Under the onslaught of weather, nothing at Bryce remains the same for long. The canyon is one of the best places on the planet to observe the forces that shape the surface of the earth.

A single summer cloudburst can carry off thousands of tons of gravel, sand, and silt to the Paria River and then on to the Colorado River and into the Grand Canyon. Bryce is changing at a fantastic rate: Its rim is receding one foot every 65 years. The place is an open textbook of geology.

Sixty million years ago, a vast body of water, called Lake Flagstaff today, covered southwestern Utah. As the ages passed, sediments of gravel, sand, and mud accumulated to thicknesses of 2,000 feet or more beneath the sea. Eventually, cemented together by minerals and pressure, the sediments turned into solid rock, which is now called the Wasatch Formation.

Above: Thor's Hammer, one of the hundreds of limestone spires, or hoodoos, scuplted by ice and water just below Sunset Point.

Left: Snowfall temporarily softens the rugged terrain above the canyon floor. When the snow begins to melt, ice and water will carry away another layer of pink cliffs, revealing ever sharper profiles.

BRYCE AMPHITHEATER

Bryce Amphitheater is the most delectable of the giant shell-shaped bites taken out of the Paunsaugunt Plateau. Several spectacular trails lead down below its rim into a wonderland of rock sculpture.

The Peekaboo Loop Trail goes from Bryce Point into the heart of the amphitheater, where the mystery and magic of the Bryce escarpment are at their greatest. As you walk down into the canyon, a formation called the Wall of Windows appears above you. This monstrous slab of limestone has been punctured with gaping holes that let the bright blue sky show through. Below you, there is a fantastic array of natural rock carvings that resembles the guests and attendants at a fancy masked ball. The dancers, waiters, musicians, and jesters are presided over by a trio of red-cloaked figures.

Farther on, a broad span of yawning cave mouths, called The Grottos, appears just beneath the rim. The caves have been carved out by water seeping down from the plateau above. Virtually inaccessible to people, the caves offer refuge to red-tailed hawks, ravens, and golden eagles. In the canyon, it is easy to get the feeling that this vast piece of the earth was pried open for your personal inspection.

Right: Visitors to Bryce never forget the unique intensity of light reflected by dazzling red sandstone against the bright blue sky.

Opposite: The rugged terrain of Silent City viewed from Sunset Point; Ebenzer Bryce, the Mormon settler for whom the park is named, is said to have described the region as "a hell of a place to lose a cow!"

Beginning about 16 million years ago, colossal movements of the earth's crust forced the formation upward. This stress produced great breaks in the rock. One of these chunks is the Paunsaugunt Plateau. The fracturing of the rock on the eastern side of the plateau, where Bryce is situated, left it particularly vulnerable to the forces of weather, especially to the slow, steady power of water. These powerful erosive forces are most on display in late winter and early spring. As the ground thaws on warm days, you can hear the grinding, groaning, and grumbling of erosion at work. Water runs down crevices, rocks tumble, and gravel and pebbles shake loose from the sides of the canyon's weird formations.

In Bryce, the endless power of erosion has sculpted thousands of the limestone hoodoos. Derived from the word "voodoo," the term means "bad luck," but in Bryce Canyon, hoodoo invokes only the benevolent magic of wondrous shapes and colors.

The stunning terra-cotta, yellow, pink, and mauve of the canyon's rock formations result from oxidized chemicals in the stone: Red and yellow come from iron; blue and purple, from manganese. Light also affects the colors of the formations in Bryce. The colors change throughout the day, moving from the blue end of the spectrum in the morning light toward red hues at sunset.

There are 13 overlooks that survey this wonderland. One of the best is Yovimpa Point, a magical rock spur nearly two miles above sea level. From here, more than 3,000 square miles of desert fall away to the south. To the east, there is a broad sweep of mesas and buttes; to the north, the Aquarius Plateau; and to the south, a descriptively named peak called Mollie's Nipple.

BRYCE IN WINTER

Every winter, Bryce Canyon becomes a fairyland. Its thousands of rock hoodoos take on the appearance of magical figures made of red and orange with mantles of white. The park service clears the 15-mile-long scenic drive to Rainbow Point, making this winter wonderland accessible by car.

With a permit, snowshoers and cross-country skiers can sleep out-of-doors in designated winter campsites along the Fairyland Loop Trail, the Under-the-Rim Trail (which connects with many of Bryce's shorter paths), and the Riggs Spring Loop Trail. Snowshoes are provided at no cost at the visitor center.

Cross-country skiers cruise along the rim through manzanita, piñon, and ponderosa pines. Skiers who don't mind getting a little snow down their collars venture down the steep trails leading to the canyon floor. There is also winter hiking below the rim for those willing to posthole up to their hips through Utah's deep light powder in exchange for some of the most spectacular winter scenery anywhere on earth.

BRYCE CANYON NATIONAL PARK

Established: 1924

Location: Utah

When to go: Open all year

Size: 35,835 acres

Terrain: Forested canyon rim and deep escarpment

Highlights: Silent City, Wall of Windows, and Queen Victoria

Wildlife: Mule deer, small mammals, reptiles, hawks, golden eagles, and other birds

Activities: Ranger-led walks and talks, evening programs, night sky programs, moonlight walks, and snowshoe walks; horseback trail rides, hiking, cross-country skiing, snowshoeing, and backpacking (by permit)

Services: Visitor center, park lodge, and two campgrounds

Information: Bryce Canyon National Park, Utah 84717; 801-834-5322

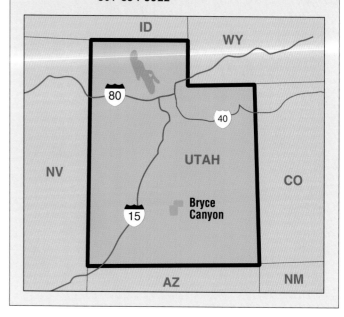

CANYONLANDS

Geological Wonderland

Canyonlands encompasses a vast sandstone wilderness cut by great chasms and gorges. From all appearances, this is one of the most arid places on earth, yet it was forged by water. The combined energy of two unusually abrasive rivers has created what is surely one of the most spectacular examples of the power of erosion anywhere on earth.

This is a landscape of deep-shadowed canyons, bright orange mesas, great buff-colored pinnacles, and maroon buttes—an intense pallet of natural colors that comes alive in the rays of the setting sun. The terrain here seems so surreal that it looks as though it might have been painted by Salvador Dali.

The wild array of arches, sandstone pillars and needles, canyon mazes, and scarps that make up the otherworldly terrain of Canyonlands National Park is the work of the Colorado and Green rivers. They meet in the heart of the park at a spectacular site called the Confluence. Here, the rivers form a great Y, cutting 1,000 feet into the brilliantly hued sandstone. From the Confluence, the rivers roll on as one.

Over the 20 million years of its existence, the Colorado River has carried away solid rock from an area the size of Texas and two miles deep. The abrasive power of this sediment, helped by wind, precipitation, and frost, has carved out

deep canyons, stark mesas, and high buttes unlike any seen elsewhere on earth.

The remarkable stripes that run through the nearly unbelievable shapes of these figures are the result of the way in which different kinds of stone have resisted the constant aggression of these natural sculpting agents. The perpendicular landscape of the region was also shaped by underlying deposits of salt. Under great pressure from the rock above, the salt is formed into huge domes that eventually fracture the surface.

The two rivers that flow together in the park divide it into three sections. In the north, a high mesa called Island in the Sky rises 2,000 feet as a great scarp several miles from the Confluence. In the east is the district known as the Needles.

Above: The Anasazi occupied the area from about the first to fourteenth centuries, leaving an abundance of rock art, such as these petroglyphs at Newspaper Rock State Park.

Left: A raven perches atop Mesa Arch, illuminated by the warm glow of sunrise. The span frames a spectacular view of sandstone spires and the La Sal Mountains.

Canyonlands: Geological Wonderland

Here, giant pinnacles banded with alternating white and red stone rise 400 feet above the grassy floors of valleys ringed by perpendicular cliffs.

Across the conjunction of the rivers, to the west, lies the Maze, an isolated wedge of canyon country. At the end of a 14-mile trail, the Maze Overlook offers a spectacular vista of rivers, spires, clefts, and canyons. Many people argue that this is the finest view in the Southwest.

Canyonlands is mostly wilderness, with paved highways penetrating only its periphery. Trails and jeep roads lead into some of its most scenic and geologically flamboyant places. They meander along the rims of high plateaus, then plunge dramatically down steep canyon walls where the descent or ascent can be as great as 40 percent. As you drop into Canyonlands, the ground falls away from you in giant stair steps; flat benchlands end abruptly in rock walls.

The eerie look of the terrain caused writer Edward Abbey to describe Canyonlands as the "most arid, most hostile, most lonesome, most grim, bleak, barren, desolate, and savage quarter of the state of Utah—the best part by far."

Below: The Needles began as rectangular blocks of Cedar Mesa sandstone. Over time, erosion widened the gaps between the blocks, creating slender spires and hoodoos.

THE NEEDLES

Visitors without a four-wheel-drive vehicle can get a real feel for Canyonlands by driving into the Needles area on the eastern side of the park. Here is a spectacular landscape of deep canyons, unusual flat-bottomed valleys, called grabens; sandstone formations, such as the descriptively named Molar Rock; and numerous arches.

An 18-mile-long paved road, with dirt spurs, leads into the area. It begins at Squaw Flat, a grassy area with piñon pine trees and junipers. At Pothole Point you can walk to rock depressions that fill with rain water. These little ponds are an important source of water in canyon country. They often teem with life, such as snails, fairy shrimp, and worms, which live through the dry summer months wrapped like mummies in dried mud.

From Pothole Point you follow the road to its destination at Big Spring Canyon. Here, squat pedestals of sandstone rise like mushrooms from the barren bedrock. This point is the beginning of the trail that leads to Confluence Overlook, one of the most spectacular trails in the Southwest. The trail climbs the side of a canyon by means of a ladder, ending at a site more than 900 feet above the point where the rivers merge.

Left: The opening in Angel Arch in Salt Creek Canyon is an exhilarating 160 feet high, but its name doesn't refer to a celestial portal. Someone thought the arch looked like a winged angel leaning against a harp.

CANYONLANDS PICTOGRAPHS

Canyonlands' pictographs (paintings on stone walls) are found in a detached section of the park called the Horseshoe Canyon Unit.

At Ghost Gallery, ancient figures painted in red ocher stare at you through the centuries with hollow eyes. Archaeologists believe that these life-size pictographs may be 6,000 years old. They do not look like the work of the Anasazi or any of the other people known to have lived in this region, so archaeologists surmise that the pictographs were left by earlier people. No one knows for sure.

More recent inhabitants of Canyonlands have also left behind reminders of their presence. These people were related to the Anasazi of Mesa Verde in Colorado and Chaco Canyon, a vast pueblo in western New Mexico. In Canyonlands, they farmed and gathered plants. In the Needles area, you can still see a small but well-preserved granary used to store corn 700 years ago.

Above: From Grand View Point, a vast panorama of rocks and canyons stretches out toward the horizon.

Opposite: The park sprawls across more than 2,500 square miles of dramatically eroded canyons, cliffs, hoodoos, and mesas around the confluence of the Green and Colorado rivers.

CANYONLANDS NATIONAL PARK

Established: 1964

Location: Utah

When to go: Open all year (the best seasons are spring and fall)

Size: 337,570 acres

Terrain: Desert canyonland, buttes, mesas, and rivers

Highlights: The Needles and Horseshoe Canyon pictographs

Wildlife: Small desert mammals and reptiles

Activities: Ranger-led walks and talks; hiking, boating, rafting, bicycling, horseback riding, fishing, four-wheel-drive tours, river-running trips, and backpacking (by permit)

Services: Four visitor centers and two campgrounds

Information: Canyonlands National Park, 2282 Southwest Resource Blvd., Moab, Utah 84532; 801-259-7164

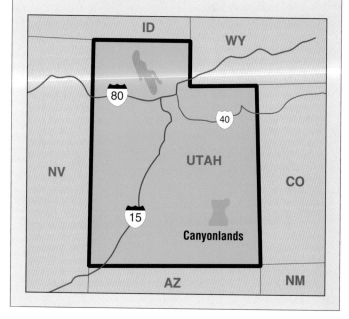

CAPITOL REEF

The Land Rose Up

From a distance it looks like a swell of gigantic ocean waves, but the Waterpocket Fold, of which Capitol Reef is a part, is an immense pleat in the earth's crust that rises in great parallel ridges for 100 miles across the starkly beautiful desert landscape of southern Utah.

The awe-inspiring formation is not actually a reef, but a ridge of limestone that once existed in an ocean. Waterpocket Fold is one of the world's largest and finest monoclinal flexures. In these unusual places, the earth's crust has buckled upwards. Early pioneers, who were not geologists, called any rocky barrier to their travel a reef, and this reef's sheer cliffs, which are nearly 1,000 feet high in some places, blocked the east-west travel in this region for decades.

Over the centuries, the exposed edges of the uplift have eroded into a slickrock wilderness that encompasses most of the park's scenic splendors. Layer upon layer of brightly colored sandstone is cut by deep, serpentine canyons or eroded into natural bridges or massive domes. One of these great monolithic rock structures apparently reminded an early traveler of the capitol dome in Washington, D.C., and he came up with the name Capitol Reef.

The park is in such a remote corner of the Colorado Plateau that the nearest traffic light is about 80 miles away. But for centuries, Capitol Reef has been known as a place of dramatic beauty that has drawn visitors to gaze at its wonders or reap its bounty. Ancient petroglyphs, often figures of bighorn sheep and other animals, were cut into rock walls by people who inhabited this area more than 700 years ago. The people who carved these figures once plowed fields in the cen-

tral area of today's park, where towering cliffs contrast with a green oasis along the Fremont River.

In the nineteenth century, Mormon pioneers farmed and planted orchards in the valley, leaving behind the apple, peach, and apricot trees that are still there to this day.

The last residents left in the early 1960s, but cattle drives through the park still bring back the feeling of the frontier days. In the southern end of the park, wilderness trails wind through places with such poetic names as Muley Twist Canyon. This path is so narrow that, in pioneer days, mules had to slither through the canyon.

Elsewhere the pioneers descriptively dubbed the terrain Poverty Flat, Fern's Nipple, Tarantula Mesa, and Dogwater

Above: The same natural forces that formed the arches in Canyonlands and Arches shaped Hickman Bridge, one of two arches in Capitol Reef.

Opposite: Fringed by cottonwood trees, the Fremont River courses through a gorge of layered sandstone.

Creek. To the north, the lovely Cathedral Valley reveals eroded spires of Entrada sandstone that rise 50 stories from the valley floor. In Cathedral Valley, a narrow four-wheel-drive road loops among stark and bizarre formations with such names as the Gypsum Sinkhole, the Walls of Jericho, and the Temple of the Sun.

Sometimes lucky park visitors encounter a herd of desert bighorn sheep. The last sighting of a native bighorn was in 1948, and park officials believe that they disappeared because of diseases caught from domestic sheep. The park reintroduced the desert bighorn in 1984.

Opposite:
Adventurous visitors will find stunning views of Hall Creek Valley and the Waterpocket Fold in the remote southern tip of the park.

CAPITOL REEF SCENIC DRIVE

Capitol Reef's lovely, 25-mile-long scenic drive leads into the heart of the park along an old wagon trail called the Blue Dugway.

Legend has it that this road has been used by Native Americans, outlaws, miners, and gypsies. It is said that the Devil himself was once spotted strolling on the trail. A pioneer farmer supposedly drove him away with the Book of Mormon. Today the Blue Dugway is graded and covered. It connects the former Mormon community of Fruita with the section of the Waterpocket Fold called Capitol Reef.

One spur road leads into the Grand Wash, a canyon supposedly used as a hideout by the famous outlaw Butch Cassidy. From the trailhead in the canyon, a spectacular hiking trail leads down to the Fremont River through a series of narrows, while another trail climbs for a mile up to an imposing rock formation known as Cassidy Arch.

CAPITOL REEF NATIONAL PARK

Established: 1971

Location: Utah

When to go: Open all year

Size: 241,904 acres

Terrain: High desert ridges, canyons, and river valleys

Highlights: Muley Twist Canyon and Cassidy Arch

Wildlife: Desert bighorn sheep, mule deer, small mammals, reptiles, and birds

Activities: Ranger-led nature walks and evening programs; interpretive exhibits, scenic drives, hiking, fruit picking, birdwatching, horseback trips, jeep tours, and backpacking (by permit)

Services: Visitor center and three campgrounds

Information: Capitol Reef National Park, Torrey, Utah 84775; 801-425-3791

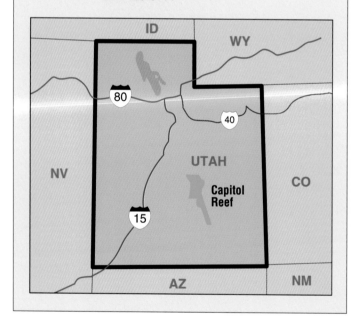

CARLSBAD CAVERNS

Sculpture Beneath the Desert

Every sunset on summer evenings, in a corner of the Guadalupe Mountains in southern New Mexico, a dark cloud swirls out of the ground; what looks like a tornado is actually half a million bats flying out of an immense opening in the earth. The bats fan out over an area 100 miles wide, catching and devouring flying insects. At dawn they return to their home.

This nightly exodus of Mexican free-tailed bats led to the modern rediscovery of Carlsbad Caverns around 1900. This great cave is one of the largest caverns in the world. The size and boldness of its huge vaulted underground chambers are truly awesome. The cave contains formations of such startling shapes and colors, and of such monumental proportions, that country humorist Will Rogers called this underground wonderland "the Grand Canyon with a roof on it."

People have known about these spectacular caverns for thousands of years. According to archaeological evidence, nomadic hunters and gatherers used the cave's enormous mouth for shelter. Apparently, they did not penetrate far inside. Shortly after its turn-of-the-century discovery, miners began excavating the cave for its huge deposits of bat guano, which was shipped to southern California for use as a fertilizer in citrus groves.

One miner, a young local man named James Larkin White, was so intrigued by the cave that he undertook a serious exploration of the labyrinthine caverns beyond Bat Cave. His passionate interest in the cave garnered the publicity that helped establish Carlsbad Caverns as a national monument in 1923 and a national park seven years later. White served as its chief ranger.

The full extent of the caverns has still not been fully explored. To date, approximately 20 miles have been investigated and mapped. Three of the most spectacular miles, which include the great vaulted chambers known as the King's Palace, Queen's Chamber, and Green Lake Room, are open to park visitors. Throughout the caverns there is a profusion of multicolored rock formations, such as the Iceberg, Boneyard, and Rock of Ages, that owe their startling hues to iron oxide deposits.

The same reef that forms the Guadalupe Mountains also spawned Carlsbad Caverns. Over time, fractures in the ancient limestone sedimentation appeared, allowing mineral-laden water to cut through the rock and form the caverns.

The cave's stunning interior decoration is also the work of limestone-carrying water. Over the millennia, dripping water has built a nearly unbelievable array of formations. Some are six stories tall; others are as delicate as lace.

Above: Each night, a cloud of 250,000 bats flies out of the gaping natural entrance to Carlsbad Caverns and spreads out across the desert in search of flying insects.

Opposite: Draped with a "flow" of crystals, a stalagmite known as the Christmas Tree stands in Slaughter Canyon Cave, which adventurous visitors can explore on special ranger-led tours.

THE BIG ROOM

When you ride an elevator into the depths of Carlsbad Caverns or walk down well-made trails into the cave, remember that the first visitors descended into the caverns in guano buckets lowered by pulleys. Tours used to begin in the uppermost of the cave's three largest chambers, the Bat Cave, but this area is now closed to everyone except the bats.

At a level 750 feet below the surface, the Hall of the Giants contains the cavern's biggest stalagmites: the Rock of Ages, Giant Dome, and Twin Domes. These monster monoliths seem to be straining toward the great vaulted ceiling hundreds of feet above them. On this level you can also tour the Boneyard, which is filled with structures that only slightly resemble bones, and Iceberg Rock, by conservative estimates a 100,000-ton hunk of stone.

Everything else within the caverns is dwarfed by the Big Room, the largest known underground chamber in the Western Hemisphere. This immense enclosure is 1,800 feet long and up to 1,100 feet wide. It is so vast that it could contain more than a dozen football fields; it is so tall that you could build a 30-story building inside it.

At the 830-foot level are other large rooms: the King's Palace, with its statuesque stalagmites, and the lovely Queen's Chamber, with rock that seems to flow like draperies. The Park Service used to affix names to the cavern's rock formations, but rangers have removed most of the labels. Now you can let your imagination work its own wonders. What do you think these weird and improbable formations resemble? A ship? A wedding cake? A Japanese garden?

Opposite:
Stalagmites and other cave formations are created by the slow, drop-by-drop accumulation of calcite crystals.

CARLSBAD CAVERNS NATIONAL PARK

Established: 1930

Location: New Mexico

When to go: Open all year, except Christmas Day

Size: 46,766 acres

Terrain: Desert mountains and caverns

Highlights: The Rock of Ages and the Big Room

Wildlife: Mexican free-tailed bats, ground squirrels, skunks, raccoons, foxes, desert reptiles, and gold eagle

Activities: Ranger-led cavern tours, self-guided audio tours, dusk bat flight program, desert nature trail, hiking, backpacking, and picnicking

Services: Visitor center and backcountry camping

Information: Carlsbad Caverns National Park, 3225 National Parks Highway, Carlsbad, New Mexico 88220; 505-785-2232

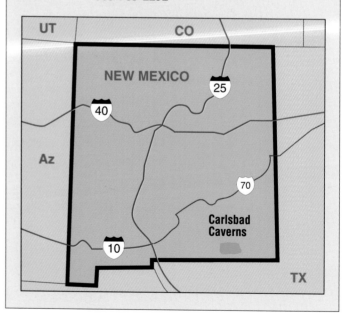

CHANNEL ISLANDS

American Galapagos

The Channel Islands jut up from the Pacific Ocean near the town of Santa Barbara in southern California. The eight offshore islands, five of which make up this unique national park, have always been intriguing.

In the past, access was limited. This gave the islands an air of mystery that was compounded by the fact that on some days the weather causes them disappear altogether, only to reappear later like distant mountains floating on a sea of clouds.

The four largest and northernmost islands—San Miguel, Santa Rosa, Santa Cruz, and Anacapa—are two to five miles apart. They are strung like great peaks of a mountain range lost long ago to the relentless sea. It takes little imagination to picture their bases on the seafloor, surrounded by foothills and valleys. The islands are volcanic remnants of an ancient mountain range that was once the western extension of the Santa Monica Mountains.

Today, only the eroded peaks rise above the ocean, but the islands were formed by the same geologic upheaval that created the mountains on the mainland. About half a million years ago, violent and extensive earthquakes gradually separated the islands from the mainland; over time, wind and water eroded them down to the outcroppings of today.

Always a sanctuary for unusual plants and animals, the islands were inhabited as early as 30,000 years ago by people who left behind a cooking pit that still contains the burned bones of a small mammoth. How people and mammoths got to the islands remains a mystery. On Santa Cruz island, there are also remnants of villages built by later inhabitants.

More recently the Chumash lived here. They went to sea in long plank canoes, caulked with tar from oil seeps, to fish and to hunt for seals, whales, and sea otters. Their peaceful existence was shattered by the arrival of the Spanish explorer Juan Rodriguez Cabrillo, who landed on San Miguel island in 1542. The Spanish hired the native people to hunt sea otters for their pelts. Over time the Spanish brought other people to the islands to help with the hunt. They warred against the Chumash, finally driving them to the mainland.

Sea otters were hunted almost to extinction to satisfy the booming European fur business. Recently they have begun thriving again on the Channel Islands, which today are a refuge for wildlife and plants found nowhere else.

Beaches, rocky harbors, and inlets provide a habitat for such exotic creatures as the northern elephant seal, which can

Above: Elephant seals like nothing better than a crowded beach. Once a seal has found a comfortable spot, it's likely to stay put for a long time.

Opposite: Seaside daisies thrive along the shores of Travertine Cove on San Miguel, one of five islands that make up Channel Islands National Park.

weigh up to three tons and wriggles up sandy beaches on its belly. An equally familiar sight is the thousands of California sea lions that return to San Miguel each year to mate, give birth, and rear their young. The islands also accommodate sea otters, northern fur seals, and all kinds of nesting sea birds.

A marine sanctuary extends for six nautical miles around each island, protecting a giant kelp forest that provides a habitat for nearly 1,000 species of fish and many unusual marine plants. Each December, great gray whales stop by the islands to feed on the bountiful sea life.

Opposite: Located on the east end of Anacapa Island about 11 miles from the California coast, Arch Rock rises some 40 feet above the water.

ANACAPA

Arch Rock rises 40 feet above the sea, hollowed out for eons by wind and water. It makes a spectacular entrance to Anacapa Island for visitors who have made the 90-minute journey by motor launch from the mainland. The formation was once part of the rocky island, but now it stands offshore as a dramatic, delicate arch.

After climbing up 154 steps from the landing platform, visitors can stroll along a one-and-a-half-mile nature trail on their own or join a park ranger for a guided tour that reveals a lot of island lore.

In many ways, Anacapa is a microcosm of the Channel Islands. Making a home here are such unusual plants as the tree sunflower, which bursts into a rich golden color in autumn. In spring and summer, thousands of wildflowers bloom here, despite the dearth of freshwater on the island. Elsewhere, there are the remnants of a Chumash midden used for cooking.

In spring, thousands of sea birds, such as petrels and oystercatchers, nest on the island's rocky cliffs high above the sea. On fine days, the nature trail offers outstanding views of the mainland from its vantage point on the cliffs more than 140 feet above the sea.

CHANNEL ISLANDS NATIONAL PARK

Established: 1980

Location: California

When to go: Open all year (access is subject to weather conditions)

Size: 249,354 acres

Terrain: Rocky islands with valleys, meadows, and dunes

Highlights: Arch Rock and Anacapa

Wildlife: Sea otters, seals, sea lions, pelicans, numerous species of sea birds, hundreds of fish species, and gray whales (December through March)

Activities: Ranger-led walks, evening programs, and wildlife- and bird-watching; tide-pool walks, swimming, snorkeling, scuba diving, fishing, hiking, whale-watching, and boat-in back-country camping (by permit)

Services: Three visitor centers (one on the mainland), three ranger stations, and three boat-in campsites

Information: Channel Islands National Park, 1901 Spinnaker Drive, Ventura, California 93001; 805-658-5730

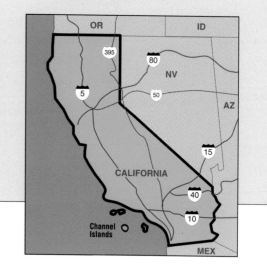

CRATER LAKE

The Bluest Water

Crater Lake in southern Oregon is a startling sight the first time you see it because of the intensity of its deep cobalt-blue waters and because of the suddenness with which it presents itself. In much the same way that the area around the Grand Canyon does not prepare you for its magnificence, the terrain surrounding Crater Lake seems an unlikely location for such a large body of water.

You approach the lake on a road that rises gradually through twists and turns up the side of a mountain clothed in forests of Shasta red fir, hemlock, and pine. Suddenly the road comes over a rise and plunges downward into a great basin, and there is the lake. At first you can hardly believe that you are seeing 25 square miles of water so blue that it looks like India Ink, circled by steep slopes, mountains, and great cliffs, which form a vast natural amphitheater.

Many of the park's features add to the spectacle of this remarkable lake. The Phantom Ship is an island made of lava, with 160-foot-high ridges and peaks that resemble an ancient sailing ship. Discovery Point is the place where on June 12, 1853, a band of prospectors looking for gold first gazed on the lake. Hillman Peak is a 70,000-year-old volcanic cone, named for one of the prospectors, and Wizard Island is a volcanic cinder cone that rises about 700 feet above the lake's surface. Its name refers to the pointed hat worn by sorcerers, which it resembles, but there is also no doubt that there is plenty of magic in this stunningly beautiful place.

One of the lake's loveliest inlets, Steel Bay, was named in honor of William Gladstone Steel. He became intrigued by the lake from a newspaper article he read while he was still

a schoolboy. As an adult, Steel worked tirelessly to make Crater Lake a national park. He lobbied for 17 years and appealed to President Theodore Roosevelt. Finally, in 1902, the nation's sixth national park was created, with the lake as its centerpiece.

The distance from the surface of the lake to its bottom is 1,932 feet, which makes it the deepest lake in the United States. Water has accumulated here over centuries as rain and snowmelt filled in a huge caldera. This vast bowl is the remnant of a volcano. Because no water flows into or out of the lake, its waters contain few minerals and almost no impurities. The lake's only fish, rainbow trout and kokanee salmon, were introduced by people.

Left: The Pinnacles were sculpted by volcanic gases and erosion. First, hot gases spewing out of tall vents solidified the rock; then erosion cut away the softer rock around the vents, leaving only the hardened spires.

Opposite: Wizard Island is a cinder cone that grew out of the crater after a blast, which may have occurred more than 6,800 years ago, created the enormous cave-in that later filled with water to become Crater Lake.

73

Scientists today still do not fully understand the ecological character of the lake. Evidence of hydrothermal venting near the lake's bottom was discovered by manned submarines in 1989. This hot water may play an important role in the lake's ecology. Recently, green algae has been found growing at a record depth of 725 feet. This indicates to scientists that sunlight may penetrate deeper in Crater Lake than in any other body of water in the world. The lake's purity and its depth also account for its startling blue color.

CREATION OF THE LAKE

How did a lake get on top of a mountain? Geologists believe the story begins long ago when a great 12,000-foot volcano, called Mount Mazama, formed as part of the chain of volcanoes in the Pacific Northwest that includes Mount Shasta and nearby Mount St. Helens.

Indian legends that relate to quarreling between the deities of heaven and the netherworld have helped geologists construct a reasonably accurate timetable. The peak was built of lava flows, ash, and debris from repeated eruptions. About 4860 B.C., Mount Mazama erupted for the last time. This gigantic explosion catapulted volcanic ash and smoke miles into the air. After the blast, Mazama's peak remained as a shell over a hollow interior. Apparently, the ancestors of the native people who knew the legend of Mazama watched the summit finally collapse with a deafening roar. This geologic event created a huge smoldering caldera.

After rain and snowmelt filled the basin, forests of hemlock, pine, and fir and meadows of wildflowers began to grow in the lava and ash on the rim of the caldera. Soon bobcats, deer, marmots, bears, hawks, and eagles arrived to make this place their home.

Opposite: In the eerie light of early morning, this lava island, named Phantom Ship, lives up to its name.

CRATER LAKE NATIONAL PARK

Established: 1902

Location: Oregon

When to go: Open all year (winter access is limited)

Size: 183,227 acres

Terrain: Volcanic caldera, lake, forests, and unusual lava formations

Highlights: Wizard Island and Phantom Ship

Wildlife: Black bears, bobcats, deer, marmots, hawks, eagles, rainbow trout, and kokanee salmon

Activities: Ranger-led walks, children's and campfire programs, historical tours, and boat tours; hiking, bicycling, fishing, snowshoeing, cross-country skiing, and backpacking (by permit)

Services: Two visitor centers, a park lodge and motel, and two campgrounds

Information: Crater Lake National Park, P.O. Box 7, Crater Lake, Oregon 97604; 503-594-2211

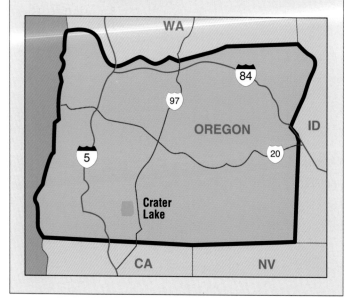

Death Valley

Forbidding Beauty

Few places are as forbidding—or as beautiful—as Death Valley National Park. Sprawling across 3.3 million acres of the Mojave Desert, the park is almost completely surrounded by mountains.

To the east, the bare walls of the Amargosa Range rise steeply from the desert floor, forming the sawtooth peaks of the Grapevine, Funeral, and Black mountains. The range is creased by dozens of deeply eroded canyons, exposing layers of pastel-colored sediments deposited millions of years ago by a series of ancient seas.

To the west, the Panamint Range rises to some 11,000 feet and is peppered with the ruins of mining camps where prospectors once searched for gold, silver, and later, borax. The mountains and canyons are still cross-hatched by old mining roads, many of them now used as hiking or four-wheel-drive trails.

This is a harsh and unforgiving land. Less than two inches of rain fall annually, much of it in brief showers that may last only a few minutes. Summer temperatures routinely soar above 110 degrees, while winter temperatures commonly dip below freezing. Expecting a heat-scorched desert, first-time visitors are often surprised to see a dusting of snow atop the highest peaks as late as March or April, when the weather on the valley floor is already quite balmy. The park's topography is equally dramatic. Elevation ranges

from 282 feet below sea level near Badwater—the lowest place in the Western Hemisphere—to 11,049 feet at Telescope Peak, where ancient bristlecone pines may be as much as 300 or 400 years old.

Between the mountains is the valley itself, about 200 miles long and as much as 16 miles across. Here, sand dunes are sculpted into ever-changing shapes by the ceaseless action of the wind; salt flats shimmer in the heat; and knobby crystal formations (such as those at the Devil's Golf Course) sparkle in the sunshine.

Left: A full moon hangs over the dessicated skeleton of a mesquite tree partially buried in the shifting, windswept sand dunes near Stovepipe Wells.

Far Left: Only salt-tolerant plants such as pickleweed grow along the banks of Salt Creek. These salty waters also sustain a rare subspecies of pupfish, *Cyprinodron salinus*, that was stranded in the valley 20,000 years ago.

On the west side of the park, the 5,475-foot peak at Dante's View overlooks the vast expanse of the valley, with its white salt sinks and scattered mesquite hummocks. Nearby, Zabriskie Point overlooks an area known as the Badlands, a broken landscape of gullies and ridges that have been gouged out of the earth by erosion.

To the north, on a dried lakebed known as Racetrack Valley, rocks leave mysterious trails across a sun-baked playa. Geologists speculate that they have been blown by powerful winds across a thin layer of ice or slippery mud. Some 30 miles away, Ubehebe Crater was blasted out of the earth's surface by a volcanic eruption about 3,000 years ago. Nearby is Scotty's Castle, a lavish Spanish-style mansion built in the 1920s by Chicago millionaire Albert M. Johnson and his companion, a "desert rat" named Walter Scott, better known as "Death Valley Scotty."

Death Valley was christened by a party of travelers who, in 1849, made a disastrous short-cut across the region to the California gold fields. Before departing, the survivors cursed the valley and gave it a name. "We took off our hats, and then, overlooking the scene of so much travail, suffering, and death, spoke the thought uppermost in our minds, saying, 'Goodbye, Death Valley.'" Today, visitors will find Death Valley much more hospitable.

SCOTTY'S CASTLE

Death Valley may seem an unlikely place for a castle, but here it is—Scotty's Castle—a two-million-dollar, 25-room fairytale palace nestled at the foot of the Grapevine Mountains.

The castle was built by a rich Chicago businessman named Albert Johnson. Advised by his doctor to find a warm, dry place to nurse his health, Johnson came to the Mojave Desert. Here, he struck up an improbable friendship with Walter Scott, a former prospector, mule wrangler, cowboy, and performer in Buffalo Bill's Wild West Show, who somehow convinced Johnson to build a retreat in an isolated canyon. Construction began in 1925 and continued for some six years until Johnson, rocked by the Great Depression, ran short of funds.

Scotty spent the rest of his long life in the mansion. He died in 1954 at the age of 84 and is buried with his dog on a nearby hillside. The Park Service offers daily tours of the castle. Although never quite finished, it is lavishly appointed with paintings, antiques, chandeliers, and a variety of imported furnishings.

Opposite: Ubehebe Crater, approximately half a mile across and more than 450 feet deep, was blasted out of the Cottonwood Mountains some 3,000 years ago by a powerful volcanic eruption.

Far Left: Rocks leave mysterious tracks on the parched lakebed of the Devil's Racetrack. One theory is that the rocks are blown by strong winds across a thin layer of water or ice.

Left: Originally named Death Valley Ranch, Scotty's Castle was built by Chicago millionaire Albert Johnson.

DEATH VALLEY NATIONAL PARK

Established: 1994

Location: California

Size: 3.3 million acres

When to go: Open all year, but summer heat can reach 130 degrees

Terrain: Desert, canyons, sand dunes, mountains

Highlights: Devil's Golf Course, Zabriskie Point, Dante's View, Artists Drive, Ubehebe Crater, and Scotty's Castle

Wildlife: Desert and migratory birds, bighorn sheep, deer, coyotes, foxes, and badgers

Activities: Ranger-led walks and slide shows, camping, hiking, cycling, bird-watching, and self-driving tours

Services: Visitor center, two museums, nine campgrounds, two resort hotels, motel, and trailer park

Information: Death Valley National Park,
P.O. Box 579,
Death Valley, CA 92328;
619-786-2331

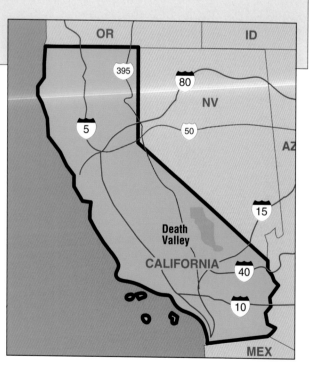

Right: The forbidding terrain of the Devil's Golf Course is formed by sodium chloride crystals—common salt—left behind by evaporating water.

DENALI

The Great One

This park and the entire wild, rugged region that surrounds it pay homage to a single geological entity: Mount McKinley, or Denali ("the Great One"), as native Alaskans call it. At 20,320 feet above sea level, this magnificent mountain is North America's highest peak and one of the grand mountains of the world.

Denali's sheer bulk and the immense rise of its perpetually white-mantled summit make it look like a monument left by ancient gods. From base to summit, McKinley is the biggest mountain in the world. Its awesome north face rises 18,000 feet to its summit from a 2,000-foot subarctic plateau. Like the Grand Canyon, Denali is one of the great spectacles of the American landscape, a sight that, once seen, will never be forgotten.

When the clouds cooperate, which is only about half the time in summer, Mount McKinley presents an overpowering spectacle. At midday the great peak sparkles as the bright sun glints off the snow and glaciers that cover its flanks from bottom to top.

At sunrise or during the long subarctic twilight, the great mountain is almost beyond belief. It becomes a magnificent mass of granite, ice, and snow enshrouded in delicate pastel shades of pink, mauve, and purple, which change with the slow movement of the sun.

The shifting light makes the mountain look deceptively soft and ethereal.

The park that encompasses the mountain and its surrounding peaks in the Alaska Range is a huge wilderness tapestry that is larger than the state of Connecticut. The mountains here, unlike the Rockies and the Sierra Nevada, are not covered with forests, because in northern latitudes the timberline falls between 2,000 and 3,000 feet instead of 11,000 to 12,000 feet. This means that most of the park is treeless. It is a broad open landscape that creates a feeling of vastness that can be overwhelming.

There are two worlds of Denali: the raw alpine region of the high mountains and the tundra-covered lowlands. Connecting one to the other are the great glaciers that flow down from the

Above: A male caribou, a member of the reindeer family, bounds over the tundra. The semiannual caribou migration is one of the great spectacles of North American wildlife.

Left: For eight months the land of the great mountain is shrouded in snow, but June brings weather warm enough to initiate a brief growing season that greens the lower elevations.

Denali: The Great One

Right: A favorite of outdoor photographers for obvious reasons, Reflection Pond is home to a rich variety of Alaskan wildlife, including moose, beavers, muskrats, and waterfowl such as loons and grebes.

Opposite: Surrounded by dense stands of spruce and aspen, Horseshoe Lake, once an oxbow of the Nenana River, may be reached on a moderate trail less than two miles from the park hotel.

summits of McKinley and the other peaks. For decades the main travel route into the mountains has been the Muldrow Glacier, an immense river of ice fed by the Harper, Brooks, and Taleika glaciers. Each originates in cirques (glacier-gouged rock basins) high on the mountain.

The ice that becomes the Muldrow begins just below the peak's summit and flows northeastward 35 miles through a granite gorge on the side of the mountain to its leading edge, or snout. On the tundra far below the summit, the ice melts, feeding the McKinley River.

Twice in the past century, for reasons not fully understood, the glacier has surged forward. The last time was during the winter of 1956-57, when the Muldrow's snout suddenly advanced five miles across the tundra. Its movement was ac-

companied by the constant sound of breaking ice and rushing water. Despite the debris and jumbled ice left by the Muldrow's last leap forward, the glacier is still used as a major climbing route up the mountain.

Denali was the first national park to be established in Alaska, and it was originally called Mount McKinley. The park was renamed in 1980, the same year the other seven national parks in the state were established by the Alaska Lands Act. Together, the eight Alaskan parks contain a staggering 41 and a half million acres, more than all the other national parks combined.

Alaska's most popular park, Denali seems unusually civilized and accessible compared with other Alaskan parks, especially Kobuk Valley and Gates of the Arctic. The Anchor-

MOUNT McKINLEY

Already the tallest mountain in North America, Mount McKinley rises a little higher each year above the tundra-covered valleys of Denali National Park.

The mountain sits atop a major geologic feature called the Denali Fault, where two of the giant plates that make up the earth's crust are colliding. The Alaska Range, along with Mount McKinley, is on the northern plate, which geologists believe is overriding the southern plate. As the two plates continue on their courses, the landmass below the mountain is pushed down as Mount McKinley itself is pushed up.

Mount McKinley has attracted mountain climbers since 1897, when it was announced that "America's rival to Everest" had been discovered. After a climb to the lower north summit in 1909 by four miners, the south summit was successfully attempted by four Alaskans, one of them a native, in 1913.

Today, most climbers try for the summit in May or early June, because after that avalanches threaten. Most climbers take a ski plane to the 7,500 level of the Kahiltna Glacier to begin the 10- to 20-day trek.

age-Fairbanks Highway (also known as the George Parks Highway) leads directly to Riley Creek Information Center on the park's eastern border, and the Alaska Railroad has a passenger station here. From this eastern gateway, a gravel road leads deep into the park's subarctic landscape.

Despite these amenities, wildlife is so visible and abundant here that Denali has been called a "subarctic Serengeti." There are shy wolves, vicious little wolverines, lumbering moose, and quick foxes, as well as countless birds and small mammals, such as the tiny pikas that inhabit the slopes.

Grizzly bears are the undisputed sovereigns of this wild terrain. They roam the park at will, feeding mainly on roots,

Right: Mantled by snow, the peak of Mount McKinley, the highest mountain in North America, is mirrored in the calm, cold surface of Wonder Lake, some 27 miles away.

berries, and other plants. When they are ravenously hungry—for instance, after a winter's hibernation—the bears may also go after arctic ground squirrels, injured caribou, or moose calves.

On a summer day, when there is up to 24 hours of sunlight, visitors to Denali see sights they will remember the rest of their lives. A huge herd of caribou migrates through a pass below Mount McKinley, heading toward its summer feeding grounds. On a green meadow on Primrose Ridge, a band of two dozen pure-white Dall sheep pause briefly as they make their way to the high alpine crags where they prefer to spend their summers. A golden eagle soars off a cliff along Polychrome Pass on the park road, while the eerie call of a loon rolls across Wonder Lake. At the same time, a grizzly takes time out to stretch and survey the surroundings while munching berries on Sable Pass, just as the clouds part to reveal the awesome bulk of Mount McKinley for one magic moment.

Right: Popular for rafting trips, the Nenana River flows swiftly beneath the snowcapped peaks of the Alaska Range along the George Parks Highway.

EXPLORING DENALI

In a park as vast as this, the opportunities for exploring are practically endless. Most visitors begin by taking the park bus on the 85-mile gravel road that extends deep into the Denali wilderness. From the visitor center on the eastern boundary of the park, the bus climbs out of a stunted spruce forest onto the treeless tundra that rolls through valleys and over gentle ridges to the flanks of Mount McKinley.

Offering stunning vistas of the Alaska Range along the way, the road winds along Primrose Ridge, then drops into marshy flats and the so-called "drunken forest" of spruce trees that lean every which way. The trees slant because of the ground's yearly freezing and thawing cycles.

After crossing three passes, the road finally reaches the Eielson Visitor Center at mile 66, a rest stop frequented by ground squirrels and even an occasional grizzly. After passing within a mile of the great snout of the Muldrow Glacier, the road comes to its terminus at the Wonder Lake Campground. The view is magnificent. If the weather cooperates you can see the sheer Wickersham Wall, McKinley's north face, which rises for more than 14,000 feet and is one of the most awesome mountain walls in the world.

Left: Dall sheep are somewhat smaller than their southern relatives, bighorn sheep, although their massive, curled horns are often larger. They are occasionally preyed upon by wolves and grizzly bears.

DENALI NATIONAL PARK

Established: 1917

Location: Alaska

When to go: Open all year (late-May to mid-September is the main season)

Size: 6,500,000 acres

Terrain: Mountains, tundra, valleys, and lakes

Highlights: Mount McKinley and Wickersham Wall

Wildlife: Grizzly bears, moose, caribou, Dall sheep, wolves, foxes, golden eagles, loons, wolverines, marmots, pikas, small mammals, and birds

Activities: Ranger-led walks, hikes, children's programs, sled-dog demonstrations, slide shows, and films; bus tours, hiking, fishing, rafting, cross-country skiing, mountain climbing, and backpacking

Services: Three visitor centers, three lodges, cabins, and seven campgrounds

Information: Denali National Park,
P.O. Box 9,
McKinley Park, Alaska 99755;
907-683-2294

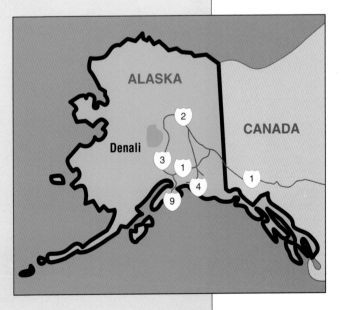

DRY TORTUGAS

Birders' Paradise

Dry Tortugas is one of the most remote national parks in the lower 48 states. Set in the Gulf of Mexico about 68 miles west of Key West, Florida, the park protects 100 square miles of sea, sand, and coral reefs around seven tiny islands known as the Dry Tortugas. Visitors may reach the park only by boat or seaplane and must bring all necessary food, water, and shelter with them.

Ponce de Leon sailed through these waters in 1513 and, noting the abundance of sea turtles, named them *Las Tortugas*. They later became known as the Dry Tortugas, owing to the lack of fresh water.

In 1840s, the United States government chose one of the islands—Garden Key—as the site of a massive fortification (the largest coastal fort in the country) designed to control access to the Gulf of Mexico. Construction of Fort Jefferson was begun in 1846 and continued for 30 years but was never completed.

During the Civil War, it was used as a military prison by the Union Army. Among its most infamous inmates was Samuel Mudd, the doctor who set the broken leg of John Wilkes Booth after the assassination of President Abraham Lincoln. The fort was abandoned in 1874, and the island and surrounding area were declared a wildlife refuge in 1908.

The fort's brick walls—some of them eight feet thick and 50 feet high—and the ruins of several buildings may be viewed on a self-guiding tour. Garden Key also offers a small visitor center, a boat pier, and the park's only campground.

Beyond Garden Key, the park is a wonderland of warm, azure water, white sandy beaches, and coral reefs brimming

with life. Snorkeling, scuba diving, fishing, and bird-watching are the main pursuits here. Opportunities abound for even a casual visitor to don a diving mask and snorkel to explore the rainbow world under the waves.

Built up over hundreds of thousands of years by tiny calcium-producing polyps, coral reefs attract a stunning variety of sea life. Among the many colorful species one is likely to see are blue-and-yellow-striped grunts, red or turquoise parrotfish, flat angelfish, trumpetfish, and prowling sharks and barracudas.

Staghorn and elk coral reach for the sunlight, sea fans wave gracefully, green turtles and loggerheads paddle lazily through the waves, and schools of brilliant blue tangs dart safely out of reach. Experienced divers may also explore more than a dozen shipwrecks within the boundaries of the park, some dating back to the late seventeenth century.

There is an abundance of wildlife above the surface, too. Situated on a main flyway between North and South America,

Above: Fort Jefferson, the largest coastal fort in the United States, occupies most of Garden Key and now houses the park's visitor center.

Opposite: The Dry Tortugas were declared a wildlife refuge by President Theodore Roosevelt in 1908. Fort Jefferson National Monument was created in 1935; it was upgraded to a national park in 1992.

the Tortugas are a major stopover for migratory birds, some of which travel as far north as Canada and even Alaska. Dozens of species may be seen in a single day in the park during the height of the spring and fall migrations. At times, more than 100,000 birds—mostly sooty terns and brown noddies—come to the islands to lay their eggs.

Sea turtles also deposit eggs on the islands. As many as two or three times each year, females haul themselves onto the beach, dig a hole in the sand with their powerful flippers, and lay about a hundred golf-ball-sized eggs. Only a fraction of the hatchlings survive; most are eaten by other animals. The survivors return to the sea and take their place in the cycle of life that keeps this fragile ecosystem healthy.

THE BIRDS OF DRY TORTUGAS

Dry Tortugas offers some of the best bird-watching in the eastern United States. Thousands of migratory birds pass through the islands or spend the winter here, resting, feeding, and sometimes nesting before their return flight to the north.

It's not uncommon for an observant birder to see a hundred species in a single day during the peak of the migration season. Among the dozens of birds that may be sighted are diminutive western sandpipers, double-crested cormorants, masked boobies, peregrine falcons, roseate terns, brown pelicans, soaring frigate birds with seven-foot wingspans, and a wide variety of warblers.

One of the most dramatic events in the park occurs in February, when 100,000 sooty terns nest on Bush Key. Females lay their eggs on the sand and take turns protecting them with the males. The birds stay in the Tortugas until the young are old enough to migrate on their own.

Although Bush Key is closed to visitors during the nesting season, the rookery may be observed from the fort on neighboring Garden Key.

Right: Though beautiful, the clear blue waters of the Tortugas can be treacherous. Shipwrecks are found throughout the park. The first lighthouse was built on Garden Key in 1825; a second, on Loggerhead Key, was added in 1856.

Left: The ruins of several structures—including the officers' quarters, soldiers' barracks, and magazine—are preserved by the fort's parade ground.

DRY TORTUGAS NATIONAL PARK

Established: 1992

Location: Florida

When to go: Open all year

Size: 64,700 acres; land area: 39 acres

Terrain: Seven islands, coral reefs, and 100 square miles of the Gulf of Mexico

Highlights: Fort Jefferson and Garden Key

Wildlife: Migratory birds, sea turtles, and saltwater fish

Activities: Snorkeling, scuba diving, fishing, bird-watching, and camping

Services: Visitor center, boat pier, and campground

Information: Dry Tortugas National Park,
40001 State Rd. 9336,
Homestead, FL 33034;
305-242-7700

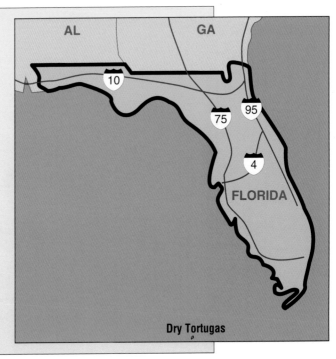

EVERGLADES

Wetland Wonderland

When you see a crocodile surging through the turgid waters of a mangrove swamp, its tapered snout sprouting enormous fangs and its great knobby back looking like some kind of moving island, fascination almost overcomes your fear. These great reptiles are unchallenged sovereigns in their wetland domain.

When a crocodile wants its progress unimpeded by other animals, or the few brave people who dare venture into its territory deep within the swamps, it gives the water a loud, angry whack with its tail. The message is clear: Everyone and everything had best scurry for cover.

Everglades is the only place in the United States where crocodiles can still be found. Appropriately, the great reptile has become the symbol of Everglades National Park. Like the park, crocodiles are wild, awesome, and, ultimately, unfathomable. This is one of the world's most complex ecosystems, a seemingly endless swamp of still water, saw grass, junglelike hammocks (masses of vegetation that look like islands), mangrove forests, and thick black muck.

The park occupies the southern part of the Everglades, a great body of sluggishly moving water that is more than 5,000 square miles in size and extends from Lake Okeechobee and Big Cypress Swamp to the Gulf of Mexico. Limestone rimming the area acts as a natural barrier against the sea. This is a place so alive with plants and animals that you can almost feel the pulse of nature.

In the air, on the ground, and in the water, living wonders abound in Everglades. The mix of plant and animal life is unique on our planet. This subtropical wilderness contains

more than 700 plant and 300 bird species, and it provides a haven for many endangered animals, including the great crocodiles and their smaller cousins, the alligators, along with the egret, bald eagle, Florida panther, and manatee.

Here in the swamp, there is much to be learned about the unusual adaptations and delicate balances that support the Everglades's stunning array of life. You might see white egg sacs on a branch that will soon hatch apple snails, the main food of the endangered snail kite, which has a special bill for removing the snails from their shells. Or you might learn about a fish called the gar, which has a primitive lung that allows it to live encased in mud during the dry season.

The source of all this life is water, with its cycle of flow and drought. During the wet season, from mid-April to mid-December, the Everglades becomes a river only inches deep but miles wide. It flows so slowly that its movement is all but in-

Above: Although not allowed within the boundaries of Everglades National Park, airboat rides are offered along the Tamiami Trail in neighboring Big Cypress Preserve.

Opposite: Wading birds, such as this great blue heron, once numbered in the millions. The bird population is severely threatened by pollution and the diversion of fresh water.

visible. In the dry season, during the winter months, the park's rich pulse of life slows down and awaits the new flow of water.

Every kind of life in the park, from plankton to panthers, depends upon this annual rhythm. Even people function on this natural timetable; park officials schedule most activities during the dry season, since high humidity and clouds of insects, especially mosquitos, make the wet season extremely disagreeable.

Congress created the first national parks, such as Yellowstone and Yosemite, to preserve spectacular and unusual scenery. Established in 1947, Everglades National Park was the first park specifically designated to protect a large and fragile ecosystem that was facing a grave threat from encroaching civilization. Because human activity was interfering with the yearly water cycle, this land was in extreme danger of being destroyed.

Water once flowed out of Lake Okeechobee without interference, but the rapid development of southern Florida began to overwhelm the Everglades about a century ago, when large tracts of wetland were considered potentially rich for agriculture and drained. Since then, canals, levees, and dikes have diverted more and more vital water from the Everglades to supply the needs of agribusiness, as well as commercial and residential developments.

In 1939, immense fires spread across the Everglades as the result of overdraining. During the 1960s, retaining walls were built on the south shore of Lake Okeechobee, and land has been developed in Big Cypress Swamp. This has disrupted the natural flow of water and poses a serious threat to the park's ecosystem.

Today, irrigated farmland comes right up to the park's gates. In the past few years, the number of herons in the park has dramatically declined, and there are just a few Florida panthers left out of a population that once roamed southern Florida at will.

Top: A haven for all kinds of wildlife, the subtropical wilderness is particularly appealing to birds. More than 300 species call the Everglades home.

Park officials want to purchase privately held wetlands east of the park, hoping that this will give Everglades a greater share of the water it so desperately needs. If its area can be extended, the park will be able to continue to protect this extremely fragile and extremely valuable ecosystem.

EXPLORING EVERGLADES

Despite the fact that this imposing wetland seems to go on forever, with only isolated patches of dry land, there are a number of ways to penetrate and explore the Everglades.

In addition to boats and canoes, the park also has a number of nature trails that lead into the heart of this wilderness. Gumbo-Limbo Trail is one of the quickest ways to explore the rich terrain of the park. This third-of-a-mile-long loop winds through mango trees and ends at a junglelike hammock. The little raised island of tropical hardwood trees (including several stunning strangler figs) seems to float above a spectacular sea of saw grass inhabited by flocks of herons and egrets.

The hammock's slight elevation above the surrounding water supports a startling array of life, including foxes, raccoons, snakes, deer, and birds. There are also solution holes here. These depressions in the limestone bedrock hold moisture during the dry season and become habitats for many kinds of insects and birds. As these solution holes fill with organic material, such as bird droppings, they become tiny ecosystems and may eventually become hammocks themselves.

EVERGLADES NATIONAL PARK

Established: 1947

Location: Florida

When to go: Open all year

Size: 1,507,000 acres

Terrain: Swampy area, hammocks, and saw grass prairies

Highlights: Gumbo-Limbo Trail and Shark Valley

Wildlife: Alligators, foxes, raccoons, deer, birds, fish, Florida panthers, crocodiles, and insects

Activities: Ranger-led walks, talks, hikes, and campfire evening programs; tram tours, canoe and houseboat rentals, bicycling, fishing, and backpacking

Services: Two visitor centers, information station, ranger station, park lodge, and two campgrounds

Information: Everglades National Park, P.O. Box 279, Homestead, Florida 33030; 305-247-6211

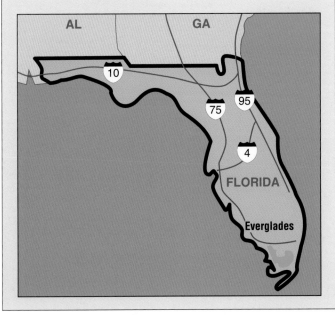

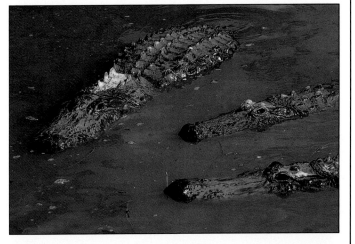

Top: Bird-watchers in Everglade National Park gather to observe a group of anhingas. The long-necked water birds dive into the water and spear fish on their sharp beaks.

Center: Alligators look something like their ancestors, the dinosaurs, but these very large reptiles are far from being extinct in Everglades National Park.

Bottom: Known as the "river of grass," the Everglades are flooded by heavy summer rains that drain into the brackish waters of Florida Bay.

99

GATES OF THE ARCTIC

The Awesome North

Some people believe that Gates of the Arctic National Park in northern Alaska is a perfect example of true American wilderness. It is a place so pure and lovely that it is the same today as it was long before people ever set foot here.

Climb almost any ridge in the park, and you will find yourself gazing upon range after range of unbelievably jagged peaks that slice into a sky filled with brooding clouds. Separated by these serrated mountains are lovely forested valleys cut by meandering rivers. This is a haunting, timeless land, where you feel deeply the call of nature and know the possibility that the valley beyond the next ridge is a place where no person has ever walked before.

The park lies entirely above the Arctic Circle and includes the heart of the awesome Brooks Range, one of the world's most northernmost mountain systems. Six hundred miles long, the great range was a mighty barrier to travel until construction of the oil pipeline and the accompanying Dalton Highway.

The vast territory of this national park—the second largest and the farthest north—embraces parts of two very different worlds. The southern slopes of the mountains are covered with scraggly black spruce forests, called *taiga*, which is Russian for "land of little sticks." These spunky trees struggle for survival in river valleys at the earth's northernmost limit for trees.

From the northern flanks of the mountains is mile after mile of treeless arctic tundra. This is a vast region of startling and unexpected contrasts. For nine months of the year, the great arctic plain is one of the most hostile places on earth. The

wind blows incessantly, and the temperature often drops to 80 degrees below zero (Fahrenheit) in the perpetual night of an Arctic winter.

Then suddenly in mid-June, with the sun above the horizon for 24 hours each day, the tundra comes alive with wildflowers. Almost everywhere, grasses and sedges, along with white reindeer moss, carpet the ground. Dwarf willows grow in jumbles where the land is soggy from the melting snow of the late arctic spring.

Along with Kobuk Valley National Park and the Noatuk National Preserve, Gates of the Arctic preserves much of the habitat of the western arctic caribou. These large deer with magnificent antlers spend their summers on the tundra, where they bear their young. With the coming of winter, the cari-

Above: Antlers are all that remain of a caribou. Sprawling across 8.5 million acres of spectacular mountains, tundra and river valleys, the park protects a vital caribou range.

Opposite: The park is filled with range after range of jagged peaks, some of which enclose forested valleys that seem lost in time.

bou migrate in herds numbering in the thousands to feeding grounds hundreds of miles to the south.

Also roaming the severe landscape in search of food are brown bears, wolves, wolverines, and foxes.

EXPLORING GATES OF THE ARCTIC

The park takes its name from conservationist Robert Marshall, who visited the area in the early 1930s. Hiking through the valley of the North Fork of the Koyukuk River in June, a month when sunlight keeps the wild land ablaze with a bright red light until 2 a.m., Marshall came upon a pair of unusually steep mountains, one on each side of the river. He called the peaks Gates of the Arctic.

"No sight or sound or smell or feeling even remotely hinted of men or their creations," Marshall would recall later. "It seemed as if time had dropped away a million years and we were back in a primordial world."

Today, visitors to the park find it as primitive as ever, a place where it is still possible to sit beneath a tree that never before sheltered a human being. Although hiking is a rewarding experience in the alpine regions of the park, rivers that have been followed for centuries by Eskimos and caribou still provide the major travel routes through Gates of the Arctic.

Six designated Wild and Scenic Rivers cascade out of high alpine valleys into forested lowlands where they become more manageable streams. Alatna River has given many visitors a stunning tour of the park. The river runs gently down from the treeless Arctic Divide in the northwest corner of the park through lovely tundra to a confluence with the Koyukuk River in a spectacular forested valley.

Opposite: The stark granite cliffs of the Brooks Range—much of which falls within the boundaries of the park—are reflected in the frigid water of the Kugrak River.

GATES OF THE ARCTIC NATIONAL PARK

Established: 1980

Location: Alaska

When to go: Summer

Size: 8,500,000 acres

Terrain: Mountains, valleys, and arctic tundra

Highlight: Gates of the Arctic

Wildlife: Caribou, brown bears, wolves, wolverines, foxes, ptarmigans, snowy owls, small mammals, and birds

Activities: Hiking, backpacking, canoeing, kayaking, rafting, fishing, hunting (with license), mountain climbing, and bird-watching

Services: One lodge

Information: Gates of the Arctic National Park, P.O. Box 74680, Fairbanks, Alaska 99707; 907-456-0281

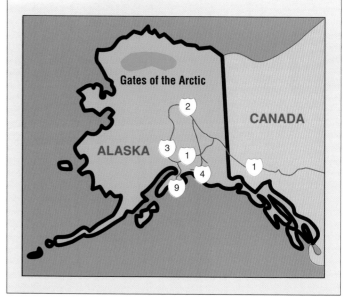

GLACIER

Sculpted by Ice

Glacier National Park presents the Rocky Mountains as you have always imagined them: granite peaks with glimmering glaciers fitted into their gorges, fields run riot with wildflowers, lakes as deep and blue as the summer sky, cascading waterfalls, grizzly bears, wooded slopes, and miles and miles of wilderness trails.

The park is the southern section of the Waterton-Glacier International Peace Park, which the United States shares with Canada. It is adorned with 200 lakes and drained by 936 miles of rivers and streams. The park is made even more magnificent by two especially graceful ranges of the northern Rockies and dozens of glaciers that seem to flow down every high mountain valley.

Glacier's 1,600 square miles, which make it about as large as the state of Delaware, offer "the best care-killing scenery on the continent," in the words of pioneer naturalist John Muir. The mountains of Glacier are not especially high when compared with those in other national parks in the Rockies, but dramatic contrasts in elevation give the park its own special grandeur.

A stunning example is the abrupt rise from the surface of Lake McDonald at 3,153 feet to the summit of Mount Cleveland at 10,466 feet. Adding to the distinctive beauty of Glacier are

the sheer faces and angular contours of its multicolored peaks, their flanks covered by heavy forests.

The area's sheltered valleys and bountiful wildlife have lured people here for more than 8,000 years. Ancient tribes tracked buffalo across the plains, fished the mountain lakes, and crossed the high passes. The Blackfeet, whose reservation adjoins the park to the east, controlled the region during the eighteenth and most of the nineteenth centuries. Straddling the Continental Divide in northern Montana, Glacier remains an unspoiled yet accessible wilderness.

An east-west scenic highway that is one of the most spectacular drives in the United States crosses the park. Called Going-to-the-Sun

Above: Hoary marmots, largest members of the marmot family, hibernate in winter. When active, they are often seen scampering on rocks above the timberline.

Left: When the warming climate stopped the forward momentum of a glacier here, it dumped some of the rocky debris it had gathered, creating the terminal moraine that later formed St. Mary Lake.

Road, it provides a highlight tour of the park's major attractions: 10-mile-long McDonald Lake, the park's largest; McDonald Falls; Avalanche Creek, where there is a trailhead for a self-guided nature walk; the precipitous Garden Wall, a section of the Continental Divide created by glaciers on both sides of its ridge; Logan Pass, atop the divide; the lovely Hanging Garden Walk; and Jackson Glacier.

This stunning wilderness realm offers more than 700 miles of trails for hiking and horseback riding. If you can find the time, you might want to follow John Muir's advice: "Give a month at least to this precious reserve. The time will not be taken from the sum of your life. Instead . . . it will make you truly immortal."

GLACIER GEOLOGY

The remnants of dozens of glaciers still cling to the walls of great rock amphitheaters, which are called cirques, in the mountains of Glacier National Park. At lower elevations, glaciers have carved out the landscape of the park from layers of sedimentary rock, consisting of mudstone, sandstone, and limestone.

The park's two chief mountain ranges, the Livingston and the Lewis, form the backbone of Glacier. They began to be thrust up about 60 million years ago. Erosion, in the form of wind, rain, snow, and flash floods, started working on these ranges about 50 million years ago. But the major carving of the mountains started about three million years ago with the Pleistocene epoch, during which four distinct glacial periods occurred. The last of these ice ages took place only 10,000 years ago.

The area of the park once contained 90 glacial remnants of this last ice age, but only about 50 remain. Two of the glaciers, Grinnell and Sperry, are easily accessible to hikers. Each is about 300 acres in size, and both are tucked into high shady hanging valleys where they continue their work of sculpturing mountains, valleys, and lakes.

Right: The magnificent Prince of Wales Hotel offers a splendid view of Upper Waterton Lake and the surrounding mountains of adjacent Waterton Lakes National Park in Canada.

PLANTS AND ANIMALS

Glacier's climate is dominated by cool, wet weather from the Pacific Northwest. The abundance of rainfall makes the forests lush, green, dense, and damp. The park's western slopes, which catch most of the moisture, are more lush than those facing east.

The vagaries of elevation and weather combine to produce four distinctive life zones within the park: grassland and prairie; the Canadian zone, with massive lodgepole-pine forests covering hundreds of square miles; the Hudsonian zone, a transition area with whitebark pine, alder, and other trees that are able to withstand long winters; and the Arctic-Alpine zone, with so-called *krummholz,* or "crooked-wood," forests of gnarled and dwarfed fir.

This unusually extensive range of topography supports a remarkable array of plants and wildlife. More than 1,000 plant species provide haven and food for 60 kinds of native animals and some 200 species of birds. Moose are the park's largest mammals. There also are white-tailed and mule deer, as well as elusive herds of elk and a variety of small mammals, such as badgers, rabbits, ground squirrels, pine martens, and coyotes. Mountain lions and rare northern Rocky Mountain gray wolves also have been spotted.

Grizzly bears, cousins of the smaller black bear, are the park's most famous residents. Considered endangered, about 600 grizzlies roam the park and neighboring wilderness lands. Distinguished by a hump on their shoulders, grizzlies generally eat grasses, berries, and roots, despite their reputation as aggressive predators.

Left: The park is laced with a network of well-maintained hiking trails, such as this one along the narrow, moss-covered walls of Avalanche Creek Gorge.

Opposite: Filled with grasses, sedges, wildflowers, and a few isolated stands of spruce or fir, Glacier's subalpine meadows provide a rich habitat for grizzly bears, bighorn sheep, and other mammals.

GLACIER NATIONAL PARK

Established: 1910 (Waterton-Glacier International Peace Park was established in 1932)

Location: Montana and Alberta, Canada

When to go: Open all year (winter access is limited)

Size: Glacier: 1,013,572 acres; Waterton: 73,800 acres

Terrain: Mountains, valleys, glaciers, lakes, forests, and prairie

Highlights: Going-to-the-Sun Road and the Garden Wall

Wildlife: Black and grizzly bears, moose, elk, deer, badgers, rabbits, squirrels, coyotes, mountain lions, and gray wolves

Activities: Ranger-led walks, campfire programs, and slide shows; climbing, hiking, horseback riding, boating, fishing, bicycling, nature courses, cross-country skiing, and backpacking

Services: Three visitor centers, seven park lodges and motels, and 13 campgrounds

Information: Glacier National Park, West Glacier, Montana 59936; 406-888-5441

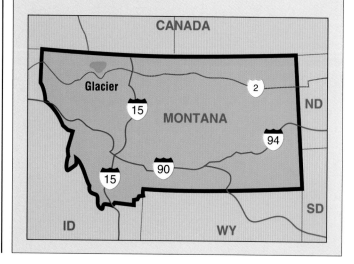

Right: The horn above Mount Clements (8,774 feet high) was created when three or more glaciers assaulted the mountain, shearing away everything but this rocky pyramid.

GLACIER BAY

The Awesome Power of Ice

Scientists think of Glacier Bay, Alaska's southernmost national park, as a living laboratory where they can study the natural processes that occur during the retreat of a glacier. The ice here is moving back from the sea at a spectacular rate; it is the fastest glacial retreat on record.

In 1794, when British sea captain George Vancouver sailed up the Alaska coast, Glacier Bay did not exist. Vancouver saw only a great wall of ice, several miles wide and thousands of feet thick, where the bay now lies. In the intervening two centuries, the ice receded more than 65 miles, leaving in its wake a spectacular fjord-rimmed bay, surrounded by forested mountains that only now are returning to life following a long hibernation.

At the southern end of the bay, where the ice first departed, the land is now covered with a lush rain forest of spruce and hemlock. Looking today as though it had been there forever, the forest of great trees, rising from a spongy moss floor, has been able to sustain rampant growth because of moisture-bearing winds from the Pacific that supply year-round precipitation. Farther north, in areas of the bay more recently deglaciated, the vegetation is sparser and the terrain more rugged.

At its head, the bay branches into two great arms, Muir Inlet and West Arm. They in turn are feathered by numerous small inlets. Alder and willow forests today grow on slopes that were covered by glaciers only 50 years ago. But at the heads of the small inlets, glaciers still calve icebergs, which drop into the water with the roar of distant cannon. This sound is called "white thunder" by the Tlingit Indians.

There are 16 tidewater glaciers that flow down from the mountains to the sea at Glacier Bay. Most of the glaciers in the park's eastern and southwestern ends are receding at rapid rates, but some glaciers on the west side are advancing. Scientists believe the depth of the water in the inlets, which affects air temperature, plays the crucial role in determining whether a glacier retreats or advances.

Here in the land of gleaming blue ice, ground that has been laid bare for only two or three decades is already starting to nourish new, although sparse, vegetation. Mosses, lichens, and mountain avens can survive on bare rock, and yellow dryad, a low-growing plant with lovely red and yellow flowers, can live in the sand and gravel left by melting ice. This diversity of emerging plant life creates a habitat for wolves, mountain goats, moose, bears, and an array of smaller wildlife.

Above: Adult and fledgling Kittiwake gulls take shelter on the sheer cliffs of Tarr Inlet in the west arm of the bay.

Opposite: Great chunks of ice break away from the face of an advancing glacier and collapse into the water with explosive force. The process, known as calving, is one of the park's most stunning sights.

113

The bay supports a food chain that begins with microscopic algae, which provide food for krill. These tiny shrimplike sea creatures are themselves fed on by the soaring fish populations. Harbor seals, with a penchant for basking in the sun on small icebergs, and harbor porpoises, nourished by this abundant sea life, make the bay their home for part of the year. At the top of the food chain are killer whales, which feed on fish and harbor seals.

The park's largest visitors, humpback whales, which are as long as 50 feet and weigh more than 40 tons, arrive each summer to cruise the waters for the tiny krill that are the mainstay of their diet. Today, the great bay is a source of endless activity both on- and offshore. This environment is less than two centuries old, but it provides fascinating viewing for human visitors.

Opposite: A view of Glacier Bay from George Island. Land and sea meet at rocky tidal zones where birds often feast on fish and other marine animals that are washed ashore by the tide.

Right: The glaciers are pulling back from the land at a rate of about one-and-a-half feet per year. This Sitka spruce, thickly hung with moss, grows on land that was under the ice 200 years ago.

GLACIERS AND ICEBERGS

The 16 glaciers that wind their way down the valleys of Glacier Bay National Park like tremendous white highways were formed during climatic periods when more snow fell during the winter than melted and evaporated in summer.

As snow builds up in layers winter after winter, its own vastly increasing weight causes the snow to compact into small grainy pellets that become crystals of ice. Eventually, this level of ice reaches such a great depth and weight that it begins to move downhill in the direction that is dictated by gravity.

The compacted ice crystals deep beneath the surface function like frozen ball bearings, gliding over one another and enabling the entire mass of ice to slide. As one of these glaciers inches its way into the waters of Glacier Bay, fissures that have developed in the ice along with the rough motion of the sea causes huge chunks to break away, or calve, with a resounding crack that can be heard miles and miles away.

THE WEST ARM

Each June, thousands of harbor seals give birth to their pups on icebergs in the small inlets at the head of the West Arm of Glacier Bay.

The icebergs provide a haven from marauding wolves and bears, but they do not always offer protection from the killer whales that glide easily through the frigid waters. Traveling in groups as large as a dozen, the whales often rise up under one of the floating maternity wards, turn it over, and dump its unwary occupants into the water, where they become easy prey.

The seals spend much of their time in Johns Hopkins Inlet. This is the wildest area of the West Arm. Here, seven huge glaciers flow down to the sea between mountains that rise 8,000 feet above the water. The other inlets of the West Arm—Tarr, Reid, and Blue Mouse Cove—offer still more spectacular scenery that includes the park's most active tidewater glaciers and its highest mountains. On clear days there are wonderful views of the distant Fairweather Range, which is capped by the mighty 15,300-foot Mount Fairweather. It is named for the only weather condition in which the peak is visible.

GLACIER BAY NATIONAL PARK

Established: 1980

Location: Alaska

When to go: Late May to mid-September

Size: 3,283,168 acres

Terrain: Bay, fjords, glaciers, and mountains

Highlight: Muir Inlet

Wildlife: Moose, wolves, black and brown bears, ptarmigans, bald eagles, salmon, harbor seals, harbor porpoises, killer and humpback whales

Activities: Ranger-led walks, films, slide shows, and evening programs; kayaking, fishing, boat tours, glacier viewing, whale and bird-watching, hiking, mountain climbing, cross-country skiing, aerial sightseeing, and backpacking

Services: Two information centers, a park lodge, and one campground

Information: Glacier Bay National Park,
Bartlett Cove,
Gustavus, Alaska 99826;
907-697-2230

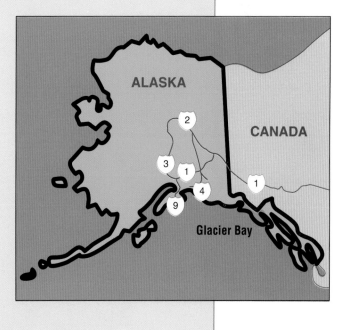

GRAND CANYON

Time and the River

The true magnificence of Grand Canyon takes all visitors by surprise. You approach the canyon from the south across a gently rising plateau, or from the north across higher and wilder country. Nothing in the topography on either side gives you a hint of what is soon to unfold.

Suddenly you are there, standing on the rim of one of the most sublime and profound spectacles on this planet. The chasm is so vast and so deep that on first sight it looks as though the earth has opened to allow us to glimpse the secrets that lie at its greatest depths.

The scale of the canyon is immense, and even from the best vantage points, only a small fraction of its 277 miles can be seen. Nobody has seen all of the Grand Canyon, despite the fact that millions of people from around the globe have been here.

Most visitors first view this truly unbelievable sight from the more accessible South Rim, which offers a stunning view into the deep inner gorge of the Colorado River. The vista is so dramatic that it can be overwhelming. What you see extending for a mile down below your feet are millions of years of geologic history. Nowhere else on earth can you view such a complete record of the geologic workings of the planet laid out so clearly and so orderly.

Some of the earth's oldest rock lies at the bottom of Grand Canyon. This rock may have formed about the same time that the first spark of life was ignited on earth. Thousands of feet thick, the rock is made up of sediments. About 300 million years after it formed, monumental geologic forces lifted the rock up into a great range of mountains that may have been six miles high, or about the height of the Himalayas. Over time the mountains eroded into a plain. About one billion years ago, that plain was raised into a second mountain range. These mountains also were worn away by millions of years of rain, wind, and frost.

During later ages, the entire region sank beneath an inland sea, with primitive shellfish fos-

Above: Mule trips are still a popular, if somewhat frightening, way to see the canyon. The animals sometimes walk perilously close to the edge.

Left: The Paiute believed that the canyon was a path to the land beyond death. For modern geologists, the Grand Canyon is a path that leads back to the planet's beginnings.

117

silizing in sea bottoms that eventually hardened to shale. Eons later, the region rose again as a high plateau; the former sea bottom was now on top and the ancient rocks below. This is when the Colorado River went to work, first cutting into the upper layers about six million years ago. Carving inch by inch over the millennia, the river finally reached the oldest rocks nearly a mile below the surface.

People lived in the canyon centuries ago, but the first white men to explore the area were 13 members of Coronado's expedition. They arrived around 1540. One wrote a letter of disgust because his expedition had encountered an unbridgeable barrier to further exploration.

In the 1850s, the army sent a surveying party into the area, but in 1869, John Wesley Powell, a one-armed army major, became the first modern player in the canyon's history. Powell set out with a small party in four boats to explore as much of the length of the Colorado River and the canyon as he could. It was an exciting journey that cost the major two of his boats. But he proved that the canyon could be explored. Accounts of his bold river run were widely published, leading to increased public interest in the Southwest. By the 1880s, a prospector named John Hance, known for a quick wit and tall tales, had begun leading sightseeing parties into the canyon.

Below: A golden eagle glides over the canyon's craggy walls. The bird's wingspan may reach seven or eight feet. An effective hunter, it preys on rabbits, rodents, and smaller birds.

Today, the national park, which was established in 1919 following years of intense campaigning, draws visitors to two major areas, its South Rim and North Rim, the latter being wilder and about 1,100 feet higher. Theodore Roosevelt called the Grand Canyon the "one great sight every American should see."

According to several surveys, most Americans—and many foreign visitors—want to see the Grand Canyon more than any other sight in the United States.

RUNNING THE COLORADO

Once you have seen the Grand Canyon from the rim and have taken in its vastness and mystery, you may get the kind of feeling about the place that has turned many onlookers into explorers. After you have had enough of the big view, you may want to see the inner canyon for yourself.

One of the most exciting ways to experience the canyon is by raft or dory trip down the Colorado. These trips vary in length from about three days by motorized raft to 18 days or more by unpowered dories, which are similar to those used by John Wesley Powell, whose journals are still used as guides by modern river runners.

Offered by a number of river companies, the trips cover long, quiet stretches of deep water through the heart of the canyon, with stops for overnight camping at several scenic or unusual sights along the way, plus day hikes to ruins, waterfalls, side canyons, and tributary streams. The river journey is broken by more than 140 major rapids. At least two of these are hand-clenching, jaw-tightening swirls of cascading water and thunderous waves that are rated 10 on a scale of 10.

Is the trip worth the challenge? Almost everybody who travels downriver through the great canyon regards it as the experience of a lifetime.

Left: Flowing southwest from the Rocky Mountains toward the Pacific Ocean, the Colorado River runs through the canyon anywhere from 3,000 to 5,000 feet below the rim.

Left: Havasu Falls plunges 100 feet over a travertine ledge into a pool of brilliant turquoise. This isolated canyon has been occupied for thousands of years by the Havasupai Indians.

Opposite: Winter quiets the Grand Canyon, spreading a thin blanket of snow over its heights and slowing the steady stream of visitors who come through the park during the rest of the year.

INTO THE CANYON

If you want a different perspective on the Grand Canyon than you can get standing on the rim, you must take one of three spectacular trails that lead down into the canyon from both the North Rim and the South Rim. The popular Bright Angel Trail winds eight miles from the South Rim down to the Phantom Ranch, a lodge and campground clustered among a glen of Fremont cottonwoods on the canyon floor.

Another alternative is the famous—or infamous, depending upon your viewpoint—muleback ride through the natural wonders of the canyon. The mules depart from the South Rim for both day trips and overnight pack trips to Phantom Ranch, where guests stay in rustic cabins and dormitories. This is the only place within the canyon itself where you can spend a night and not camp out. The ranch lies in a deep gorge of the inner canyon, near the place where Bright Angel Creek joins the Colorado River.

As you journey down into the canyon on the back of your small but sturdy mule, you will have plenty of time to observe a variety of plant and animal life that you could otherwise only see by traveling from the Sonoran Desert of Mexico to the shore of Canada's Hudson Bay. The canyon's great depth contains such a range of temperature and precipitation that the variety of local climates equals the natural scope of nearly the entire continent. These life zones mostly occur in the order you would expect, but in some places the desert zone is higher than the Canadian zone because the canyon's topography can make a high area hot and a low one cool.

Right: The sheer walls of Wotan's Throne near Cape Royale on the North Rim. With an elevation of more than 8,000 feet, the North Rim is cooler, moister, and about a thousand feet higher than the South Rim.

GRAND CANYON NATIONAL PARK

Established: 1919

Location: Arizona

When to go: Open all year (North Rim is closed late-October to mid-May)

Size: 1,218,375 acres

Terrain: High desert plateau and vast canyonland

Highlights: Phantom Ranch and North Rim

Wildlife: Bighorn sheep, deer, cottontail rabbits, Kaibab and ground squirrels, rattlesnakes, spiny lizards, small mammals, reptiles, and birds

Activities: Ranger-led nature walks, talks, slide shows, and campfire programs; horse and mule trips, hiking, bicycling, fishing, river rafting, air tours, cross-country skiing, and backpacking

Services: Two visitor centers, seven lodges, and four campgrounds

Information: Grand Canyon National Park, P.O. Box 129, Grand Canyon, Arizona 86023; 602-638-7888

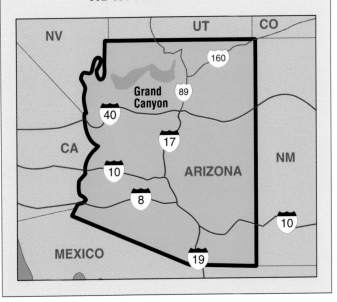

Left: Visitors can climb to the top of the 70-foot Desert View Watchtower, built in 1933 on the edge of the South Rim. Murals inside the tower were painted by Native American artist Fred Kabotie.

Opposite: Elves Chasm knifes through a canyon wall, revealing sedimentary layers deposited hundreds of millions of years ago. Small waterfalls like this support hanging gardens of ferns, mosses and wildflowers.

GRAND TETON

Awesome Mountain

The Tetons are the mountains of dreams, a rise of granite towers so impossible and impenetrable that they appear to guard a hidden land that only can be imagined but never truly attained.

The summit of Grand Teton is 13,770 feet above sea level, and the mountain shoots a mile and a half straight up into the Wyoming sky without intervening foothills. Flanked by stunning spires, pinnacles, and buttes, the steepness is breathtaking.

An early nineteenth-century French trapper supposedly named the Tetons for female breasts, which he somehow imagined they resembled. The name does not really fit, but for English-speaking Americans it has taken on a certain descriptive quality that seems to go with the mountains today.

Not particularly large at 310,000 acres (485 square miles), Grand Teton National Park encompasses the 6,300-foot-high valley called Jackson Hole, with Yellowstone to the north and the Tetons to the west. Within the park's boundaries, there is more scenery, more history, more animals, more boating and fishing, and more hiking and mountain climbing than in many areas twice its size. The Grand Teton massif, which includes five consort peaks (Middle and South Tetons, Mount Owen, Teewinot, and

Nez Perce), dominates the central part of the range. To the north, Mount Moran is a stark granite hulk 12,605 feet high. It rises in splendid isolation from the shore of Jackson Lake, the largest of six jewellike lakes strung along the base of the mountains.

Many people who visit the Tetons are surprised at their first sight of these rugged mountains. They are hypnotically alluring, and there are no bad views of them from any place in the park.

Left: The Snake River meanders gracefully through Grand Teton, illuminated by a fiery sunset. The river takes shape in Yellowstone National Park and flows more than 1,000 miles to its confluence with the Columbia River in Oregon.

Far Left: Inhabited by Indians as much as 8,000 years ago, Jackson Hole and the Tetons, reflected here in a channel of the Snake River, were explored in the early 1800s by well-known mountain men such as John Colter and Jedediah Smith.

127

Grand Teton: Awesome Mountain

Most visitors also find that they are somewhat familiar with these mountains. They have already seen them in western movies, such as the classic *Shane*, and in countless ads and television commercials. The Grand Tetons have become a recognizable symbol of the long gone American West—tough and proud.

The Snake River flows peacefully from Jackson Lake. The 30-mile-long stretch that traverses the park is braided into several channels that run through a forested, serpentine trough. It is an ideal stream for first-time river runners. Their ride down the Snake provides a unique perspective on some of America's most spectacular scenery.

Wildlife flourishes in the valley of the Snake. Bald eagles nest in dead trees alongside the stream, as do the great ospreys that cruise above the river casting their sharp eyes for the native cutthroat trout that is their favorite meal. In little side streams, moose often wade up to their knees as they placidly feed on grasses along the shore or nibble on lily pads. Along the banks, otters play, while beavers go about their business of dam building in watery alcoves and nooks.

The first people arrived in Jackson Hole long before white men set foot on the North American continent. A pointed obsidian blade found in the northern end of the park indicates a human presence as long ago as 8,500 years. The first humans who came here were probably hunters and gatherers. By 1600, Shoshone and Athapaskan people had discovered the valley.

In 1807, John Colter, a member of the Lewis and Clark expedition, wandered alone into the Yellowstone-Jackson Hole area and brought back incredible tales of exploding geysers and impenetrable mountains. The region was first named "Colter's Hell" in his honor.

The first permanent settlers arrived here sometime during the 1880s. One original homestead, a log ranch house built by the Cunningham family on the eastern side of Jackson Hole, has been maintained in the park for historical purposes. The view of the Grand Teton mountains through its kitchen window is a stunning reminder of the hardships and terrible winters the family endured beneath the very same spectacular scenery.

Below: Carved by glacial ice thousands of years ago, the Tetons' sheer-walled canyons still harbor snowfields and several small glaciers. Mountain streams swell with snowmelt in spring and early summer.

HIKING TO LAKE SOLITUDE

Hiking through a deep slice in the mountains called Cascade Canyon, just north of Grand Teton, gives visitors a good feel for some of the geological wonders of the park.

The hike starts on the west side of Jenny Lake. In the lower part of the canyon, rushing water, here and there in the form of cascading falls, seems to be constantly at work, eating away at the granite walls. Cascade Canyon originally was cut as a V by running water. Now it has been formed into a U shape, its nearly vertical sides sculpted by the powerful activity of glaciers in the last ice age.

As you walk through a series of switchbacks, granite walls rise 2,000 to 3,000 feet above you. Two miles into the canyon, the peaks tower a mile above. Abruptly, the canyon drops away, the rocky trail begins a steeper ascent into a broad bowl, and you suddenly discover that you have walked around to the north side of Grand Teton. After a total of seven miles, you arrive at Lake Solitude.

Here, in an incredibly beautiful valley, the air is intoxicatingly clear, and wildflowers, such as pink primrose and St. John's wort, abound. Grand Teton and Mount Owen are reflected in the lake, and a circular granite wall rises in the west.

Right: Aspens, cottonwoods, willows, alders, blue spruce, and other moisture-loving trees thrive on the floodplain of the Snake River below the bare pinnacles of the Teton Range.

Left: Moose, the largest member of the deer family, cross the Snake River on a frigid winter morning. The park is particularly beautiful under a mantle of newfallen snow.

131

TETON GEOLOGY

The fierce geology of the Tetons accounts for almost everything unusual about the region: the afternoon thunderstorms that can turn suddenly nasty, the deep canyons that shelter bears and deer, the broad river basin that provides grazing for moose and a refuge for elk, and the long and bitter winters. A walk into any of the canyons between the mountains reveals this geology firsthand.

The Tetons are a text-book example of fault-block mountains. This means that they were pushed up as the earth split along a north-south fault line. As pressures deep within the mantle forced the blocks on each side of the crack together, the western block rose to form the mountains and the eastern block sank to form the valley.

The granite on the summits of some of the peaks is more than three billion years old, which makes it some of the oldest rock in North America. But the mountains themselves are the youngest of the Rocky mountains. Only 12 million years old, they are mere adolescents compared with the rest of the 60-million-year-old range.

Because of their relative youth, the Tetons are more rugged than the rest of the Rockies. Since their eastern flank was the side that shoved up, this side of the mountains is more abrupt and dramatic than the somewhat gentler western side. This accounts for the fact that you have probably heard of Jackson Hole but may not know about Driggs, the Idaho town at the western base of the Tetons in a broad valley known as Pierre's Hole.

Opposite: The braided channels of the Snake River provide wetland habitat for a wide array of Rocky Mountain wildlife such as Canada geese, ducks, beavers, elk, and moose.

GRAND TETON NATIONAL PARK

Established: 1929

Location: Wyoming

When to go: Open all year (winter access is limited)

Size: 310,516 acres

Terrain: Mountains, canyons, lakes, and river valley

Highlights: Cunningham Cabin and Lake Solitude

Wildlife: Black and grizzly bears, moose, elk, deer, cutthroat trout, bald eagles, ospreys, beavers, and otters

Activities: Ranger-led nature walks, slide talks, campfire programs, tipi demonstrations, and wildlife watches; raft trips, mountain climbing, bicycling, horseback riding, fishing, ice fishing, dogsledding, cross-country skiing, and backpacking

Services: Two visitor centers, three lodges and cabins, two guest ranches, and eight campgrounds.

Information: Grand Teton National Park, Post Office Drawer 170, Moose, Wyoming 83012 307-733-2880

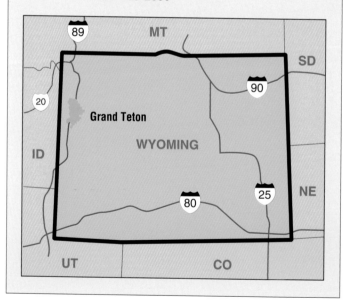

GREAT BASIN

Endless Horizon

Between the Rocky Mountains and the Sierra Nevada, in a corner of the vast territory that stretches across the West, an unexpectedly rugged landscape suddenly rises above the floor of the desert into the great blue sky of eastern Nevada.

Peaks and hills carved by glaciers from a Pleistocene ice age tower more than a mile above the flat surface. Across the forest-covered flanks of the mountains are piles of rocks left by ancient glaciers. Great Basin also holds alpine lakes, rollicking streams and rivers, and lovely green meadows filled with many varieties of wildflowers.

Great Basin was named by John C. Fremont, who led the first party of white explorers into this territory in the mid-nineteenth century. Although maps make it look like a basin, the region actually consists of more than 100 valleys. One of the newest national parks within the 50 states, Great Basin takes in only a small part of this vast expanse of land, which includes some of the nation's most geologically fascinating terrain.

Great Basin National Park offers visitors plenty of solitude, as well as sweeping views of the basin and range country that lie within and outside its boundaries. The centerpiece of the park is Wheeler Peak, Nevada's second tallest mountain at 13,063 feet. The main park road travels up to its 10,000-foot level.

From there, a trail leads to a stand of bristlecone pines, the world's oldest living trees. They look ancient indeed with their twisted, gnarled trunks and their bark carved and polished like rock by eons of wind, snow, and ice. The trees are vestiges of a Pleistocene forest that once covered the region.

Bristlecones are survivors; they continue to live even after most of their trunks and branches die, sustained by minuscule amounts of moisture. Some of the trees in the park are more than 3,000 years old; they were alive when the pharaohs ruled Egypt. One tree named Prometheus lived for nearly 5,000 years before it was cut down in 1964.

Lehman Caves is on the lower slopes of Wheeler Peak, at an altitude of around 6,800 feet. The caverns are an underground wonderland filled with intricate and spectacular formations. Rangers lead visitors through approximately one and a half miles of trails. The caverns are filled with latticed columns, undulating draperies, helicotites, and stalactites. These formations are so dense that the caves' first explorers took along sledgehammers to clear a trail.

Among its many treasures, Lehman Caves contains excellent examples of cave shields. These large and rare disks grow

Above: At the limit of the timberline, 4,000-year-old bristlecone pines survive in an incredibly hostile climate of harsh winters and lengthy annual droughts.

Opposite: The rocky, snow-covered summit of Wheeler Peak, the second highest point in Nevada, towers over a grove of aspens in the park's Inner Basin.

out of ceiling cracks where seeping mineral-laden water deposits sediments in flat circular shapes. A small community of pack rats, cave crickets, and strange spiders with scorpionlike pincers are also found in the caves.

Above: Parachute formations are unique to Lehman Cave, but no one has yet been able to explain exactly how dripping water containing calcium carbonate creates these unusual shapes.

Opposite: The calm surface of Baker Lake reflects a nearly perfect image of Pyramid Peak, one of several mountains in the Snake Range that exceed 10,000 feet.

UP WHEELER PEAK

Great Basin's only glacier lies near the 13,063-foot summit of lovely Wheeler Peak, close to a stand of bristlecone pine trees. The summit can be reached by car and by foot.

From the main park road, visitors follow a trail that leads up the mountain to the Wheeler Peak Campground. Along the way the environment changes from a piñon and juniper forest, which is able to withstand drought, to a high-altitude world of spruce, pine, and aspen. At the 10,000-foot level, visitors have a choice of several trails into the park's backcountry or a trail to the peak's summit 3,000 feet above.

One of the most popular hikes is the three-mile Alpine Lakes Loop Trail. It leads to a spectacularly scenic alpine setting, with a ragged mountain ridge rising high above a lake. Another trail follows the ridge up to the summit, which is populated by pikas and marmots and decorated with wildflowers poking out of niches in the rock.

GREAT BASIN NATIONAL PARK

Established: 1986

Location: Nevada

When to go: Open all year (winter access is limited)

Size: 77,100 acres

Terrain: High desert and alpine

Highlights: Wheeler Peak and Lehman Caves

Wildlife: Bighorn sheep, mule deer, coyotes, rattlesnakes, small mammals, and dozens of bird species

Activities: Ranger-led nature walks and talks, campfire programs, cave tours, candlelight cave tours, and spelunking trips; Wheeler Peak scenic drive, hiking, fishing, climbing, cross-country skiing, and backpacking

Services: Visitor center and four campgrounds

Information: Great Basin National Park, Baker, Nevada 89311; 702-234-7331

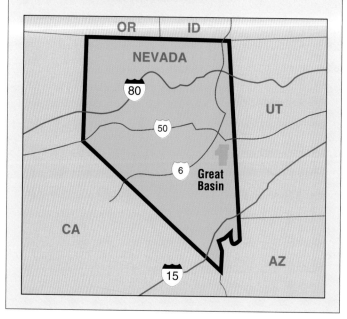

GREAT SMOKY MOUNTAINS

Heart of Appalachia

The great forest looks like a remnant of an ancient time when the world was covered with trees—a time of constant showers, fog, and endless mist. The forest floor is thick with spongy green moss and colorful wood sorrel, and everywhere there are waterfalls cascading into nooks of rivers and streams. During the summer, a riot of sound seeks your ears: the chatter of red squirrels and the calls of wrens and other birds.

Great mountains rise, ridge upon rounded ridge, beyond the horizon. Made of ancient rock uplifted from deep below the earth's surface, these behemoths are considerably older than the rough, craggy mountains of the western states. The Great Smoky Mountains are the quintessential mountains of the eastern United States. Straddling the North Carolina-Tennessee border, they preserve one of the finest deciduous forests left on earth. These ancient mountains are, in fact, among the oldest on the planet. The Smokies are also the highest range east of the Black Hills; they seem strangely out of the place so far south.

About 10,000 years ago, when glaciers advanced from the north during the last Pleistocene ice age, the mountains were already millions of years old. The glaciers cooled the climate of the Great Smokies. Lured by the

cold, northern evergreens and other plants extended their range south.

Later, as the glaciers receded, these forests also withdrew, remaining only on the heights of the Smokies where conditions were cool and moist. Throughout the park, signs advise visitors to see "the world as it once was." Because the great glaciers were stopped in their southward journey by these mountains, which include 25 peaks above 6,000 feet, the Great Smokies today harbor a unique blend of northern and southern animals and plants.

The park is truly a vestige of an age lost in the mists of time. Northern black bears roam among a profusion of southern birds, possums, and raccoons. In the great forests, rhododendron and mountain laurel grow through narrow openings

Above: A white-tailed buck leaps over a fence. The Great Smokies are a sanctuary for a diversity of wildlife, ranging from large mammals like black bears, to more than 20 different species of salamanders.

Left: Generous rainfall sustains some 2,000 plant species, among the most diverse in the world. The park has been proclaimed an International Biosphere Reserve.

in the ancient rocks. Many of the park's nearly unbelievable variety of flowers are found only here. The vegetation is so dank and dense in some places that shrubs have taken over altogether, creating jumbled areas, called "heath balds," that are too overgrown for trees to manage to survive.

Part of the Appalachian system, the Great Smokies are remarkable for their wild and luxuriant vegetation. More than 100 species of trees and more than 1,300 kinds of flowering plants grow here. The incredible tangle of trees and brush throughout the park is responsible for the "smoke" that gives the mountains their name. Water and hydrocarbons are exuded in great profusion by the close-packed array of air-breathing leaves, producing the filmy haze that never leaves this place during warm weather.

The park, which covers 800 square miles in the heart of these mountains, has so many types of eastern forest vegetation that it has been designated an International Biosphere Reserve. About half of this large lush forest is virgin growth that dates back to well before Colonial times.

Although this is our most popular national park (there are more than 900 miles of trails, including a 70-mile stretch of the Appalachian Trail), it is not necessarily the most crowded. Because the forests and mountains are so vast, entire sections of the park often seem deserted. What's more, the park is almost wholly undeveloped; much of it is barely laced by paved highways or dirt roads.

Many of the coves and valleys of the Great Smoky Mountains have been settled since the late-eighteenth century, but

Opposite: Sunlight illuminates frost-covered trees on a cold spring morning. The park's high-elevation coniferous forest is similar to the forests of the northern United States and Canada.

Right: During May, warm days dress the forest in shades of green, while flowering dogwoods sparkle with their own special iridescence.

they remained isolated and inaccessible until the twentieth century, when loggers first began harvesting the virgin timber. Still preserved within the park's boundaries are many of the cabins, farmhouses, churches, and barns of the mountain people. One of the most charming of these structures is an early nineteenth-century chapel with a small graveyard.

HIKING THE APPALACHIAN TRAIL

The Appalachian Trail, the world's longest continuous walking route, passes through 14 states, from Springer Mountain in Georgia to Mount Katahdin in Maine, along its 2,144-mile route. Hiking and trail clubs maintain shelters and campsites along the path, which was designated a national scenic trail in 1968.

The trail enters Great Smoky Mountains National Park from the south through the Cheoah Mountains and the Nantahala National Forest. Most of the 70 miles of the trail, which almost perfectly bisects the park from southwest to northeast, passes through virgin wilderness well away from highways or other trails.

From the southwest, the trail crosses near the 5,530-foot summit of Thunderhead Mountain and then follows the Tennessee-North Carolina border through a thick spruce and fir forest to the fire lookout tower on top of 6,643-foot Clingmans Dome, the park's highest point. From the tower, depending on the weather, hikers get either a stupendous panoramic view of range upon range of mountains or a swirl of churning clouds.

After the trail crosses a park highway at Newfound Gap, hikers can take a side trip through towering 200-year-old eastern hemlocks to Alum Cave Bluffs, the site of a nineteenth-century commercial alum mine and a source of saltpeter for Civil War gunpowder. After passing near the summit of 6,621-foot Mount Guyot, the trail leaves the park near the Big Creek Campground and enters Cherokee National Forest.

Top right: It's not uncommon to hear the hollow, rapid-fire tapping of the pileated woodpecker echoing through the forest. Some 200 species of birds may be found in the park throughout the year, including warblers, vireos, hawks, and owls.

Right: The park is laced with more than 800 miles of hiking trails, including a 70-mile stretch of the Appalachian Trail along the crest of the Smokies.

Left: Known as the Land of Moving Water, the Smokies receive more than 80 inches of rainfall annually, feeding dozens of cold, clear creeks and rivers.

Right: Autumn hues work their magic on the Oconaluftee River Valley, seen here from Newfound Gap Road.

GREAT SMOKY MOUNTAINS NATIONAL PARK

Established: 1934

Location: North Carolina and Tennessee

When to go: Open all year

Size: 520,269 acres

Terrain: Mountains, valleys, waterfalls, and thick deciduous forests

Highlights: Clingmans Dome, Cades Cove, and Thunderhead Mountain

Wildlife: Bears, deer, raccoons, possums, foxes, birds and salamanders

Activities: Ranger-led nature walks and children's campfire programs; auto tape tours, hiking, bicycling, fishing, horseback riding, cross-country skiing, and backpacking

Services: Two visitor centers, LeConte Lodge, and 10 campgrounds

Information: Great Smoky Moutains National Park, 107 Park HQ Road, Gatlinburg, Tennessee 37738; 615-436-1200

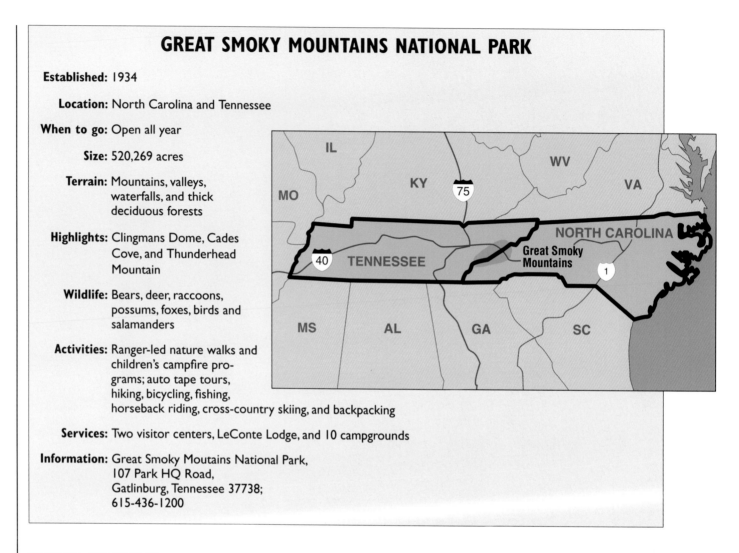

Right: Newfound Gap Road follows the Little Pigeon River as it rushes down the northern face of the Smokies into Sugarlands Valley.

Left: A glorious view from Chimney Tops. The steep trail to the summit passes through a virgin stand of hardwoods that somehow were spared from extensive logging in the early 1900s.

GUADALUPE MOUNTAINS

History in the Desert

The dry flatlands of the Chihuahan Desert, a vast, barren stretch of cactus and greasewood that extends for hundreds of miles across West Texas and south into Mexico, seem an unlikely place to find an ocean reef. But here, hundreds of miles from the nearest saltwater, an immense escarpment of orange and red limestone that was once on the bottom of a sea glistens in the bright sunlight.

The Guadalupe Mountains, a V-shaped range with its northern arm extending into New Mexico and its southern arm pointing toward Mexico, rise more than a mile above the desert. Visible for nearly 50 miles, a great monolithic rock called El Capitan, which in Spanish means "the chief," rises audaciously at the point of the V. For centuries it has been a landmark for travelers crossing this vast desert.

At more than a mile and a half above sea level, El Capitan (8,085 feet) and adjacent Guadalupe Peak (8,751 feet) are the two tallest mountains in Texas. The peaks are the most obvious sections of the Capitan Reef, most of which still lies buried thousands of feet below the desert's surface.

More than 200 million years ago, the immense reef enclosed about 10,000 square miles of a shallow inland sea. The reef was formed as the remains of lime-secreting algae and other primitive creatures that lived in the sea washed ashore. Gradually the climate of the region changed, and the sea dried up, leaving much of the reef exposed. More millennia passed, and the seabed and the reef were buried beneath a vast plain, where they remained for millions of years. Then, about 12 million years ago, geologic processes deep beneath the earth raised and tilted the ancient seabed and reef, leav-

ing the 40-mile section now known as the Guadalupe Mountains high and dry. In the process, the reef was fractured in several places.

Over more millions of years, wind and water worked to turn these deep cracks into lovely canyons that slice into the mountains we see today. These chasms, including McKittrick Canyon, Dog Canyon, and many others, are the heart of Guadalupe Mountains National Park.

Archaeological remnants, such as spear tips, knife blades, bits of basket work, and pottery shards, attest to a human presence in the Guadalupe Mountains that goes back about 12,000 years. When people first came to the area, during the decline of the last Pleistocene ice age, the climate was wet and humid. The first people who lived here probably foraged for food and hunted such animals as camels and mammoths.

By the time Spanish explorers appeared (around 1550), wandering Mescalero Apaches often made their camps at

Above: The Guadalupe Mountains are one of the world's biggest coral reefs, dating from a time when a large part of Texas was a vast saltwater basin.

Opposite: From as far away as 50 miles, El Capitan can be seen rising almost straight up out of the flat, desolate wasteland that surrounds it.

springs near the base of the range. Apache and Spanish legends about great treasures of gold and silver hidden in the mountains eventually drew American prospectors to this desert. In the years after the Civil War, they were followed by farmers, ranchers, and the U.S. Cavalry.

In the Guadalupe Mountains, the Mescalero Apaches made their last stand, but by 1890 virtually every Apache had been killed or forced onto a reservation. Initially the territory was taken over by private ranching and mining interests. Over time, enough land was donated to create a park, which is still being expanded as more land becomes available to the Park Service.

Opposite: The park's unusual formations are the result of a long and complex series of events, including faulting, erosion, and the advance and retreat of an ancient sea.

EXPLORING THE GUADALUPE MOUNTAINS

The special wonders of this national park are found in the steep contoured canyons that cut deeply into the Guadalupe Mountains.

The canyons hold forested glens of deciduous trees and alligator juniper alongside meadows of hip-high grasses and creosote plants. In Dog Canyon, among stands of Gambel oak, Douglas fir, and limber pine, you can still see Apache mescal-roasting pits.

Five miles long and thousands of feet deep, McKittrick Canyon contains an array of life and geological history unique to our planet. Amid forests of oak, juniper, maple, and the lovely Texas madrone with its oddly twisted red bark, you can find the remnants of the floor of a sea that covered the area more than 200 million years ago. Above you, inlaid in the canyon walls, are millions of years of geological history told by layers of ancient fossils and startling rock formations.

The canyon was named for Kid McKittrick, a bank robber. Legend says he hid in the canyon after fleeing from New Mexico. He was never captured, and he supposedly left a cache of loot buried somewhere in the canyon.

GUADALUPE MOUNTAINS NATIONAL PARK

Established: 1972

Location: Texas

When to go: Open all year

Size: 86,416 acres

Terrain: Mountains, canyons, and desert

Highlights: El Capitan and McKittrick Canyon

Wildlife: Mountain lions, javelinas, rattlesnakes, foxes, ground squirrels, skunks, raccoons, other small mammals, birds, and reptiles

Activities: Ranger-led walks and talks; hiking, horseback trail riding, and backpacking

Services: Two visitor centers, ranger station, and two campgrounds

Information: Guadalupe Mountains National Park, HC 60, Box 400, Salt Flat, Texas 79847; 915-828-3251

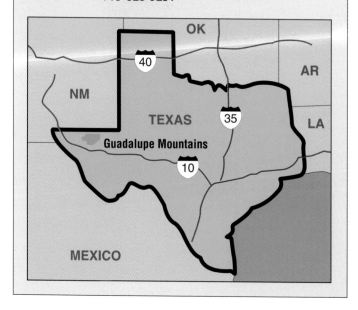

HALEAKALA

House of the Sun

Haleakala sleeps on the Hawaiian island of Maui. This huge, dormant volcano is a wild moonscape that extends for 33 miles in one direction and 24 miles in the other.

At the top of this great mountain is a 19-square-mile circular crater. Its floor, which is 2,720 feet below the summit, is a starkly beautiful and forbidding landscape of cinder cones and sculptures of lava colored with startling shades of red and yellow. Haleakala is a volcano that has grown cold, but its enormous crater is filled with unearthly shapes and profiles that are vivid reminders of its fiery past.

Light from the sun comes early to the rim of the vast crater, and it remains here long after darkness has fallen on the lower slopes of the mountain. Haleakala means "house of the sun," and according to legend, the mischievous demigod Maui tamed the sun in the great mountain's summit basin.

Long ago there were only a few hours of light each day because the sun was so lazy that it hurried home to rest. The demigod's mother was unable to dry her clothes during the few hours of sunshine, so Maui climbed to the mountain's summit, where he caught the sun by trapping its first rays as they crept over the crater's rim at dawn. He released the sun only after it promised to move more slowly across the sky.

Haleakala has not had a major eruption since about 1790, according to both Hawaiian legend and records kept by Europeans. Maps and charts made by early European explorers show significant changes in the island's topography that probably resulted from the flow of lava. But even though Haleakala is dormant, nobody would call it extinct.

Earthquakes on Maui indicate to geologists that the great volcano still rumbles far below the surface, and islanders adamantly believe the sleeping mountain will wake up breathing fire again within a century.

Haleakala's gigantic crater was not created by the kind of explosion that blew the top off Mount St. Helens in 1980. After thousands of eruptions built up the mountain from the bot-

Above: Tourists take in sweeping views of Haleakala and the surrounding area from the visitor center, perched on the edge of the crater at an elevation of 10,000 feet.

Left: Lush tropical plants like the many-armed hala tree crowd the edge of 'Ohe'o Gulch, where the waters of 'Ohe'o Stream spill into the ocean.

tom of the Pacific Ocean, a climatic change brought long-lasting torrential rains. Water flowing down the sides of the peak turned into huge rivers pouring from the summit. These raging streams cut long, deep valleys down the flanks of the mountain. The crater was created as two of the valleys joined at the mountaintop and eventually eroded it into the vast amphitheater.

Today the mountain's crater—which geologists quicky point out is not really a crater, but a canyon—is a dry, desolate terrain where it can be unbearably hot during the day and frosty cold at night. The bowl is pocked with small craters and studded with cones formed of cinder and ash. Puu O Maui, the tallest of these multicolored figures, rises 600 feet above the stark topography.

A landscape that is more inhospitable to plants and animals would be hard to imagine, but in one corner, where a break in the crater wall allows moisture to seep in on waves of clouds, leather ferns, called `ama`u, thrive along with other unusual plants. In other places you will find silversword, an endemic plant with dagger-shaped leaves that grow out in silky, symmetrical balls. This rare plant takes four to 20 years to grow to maturity, after which it sends out a single, magnificent flower stalk in a burst of summertime bloom, then withers and dies.

Although the crater is the centerpiece of the park as well as its major attraction, Haleakala also has regions of coastline and mountain desert. The park has been designated a United Nations International Biosphere Reserve.

The road to Haleakala's summit rises from close to sea level to more than 10,000 feet in just 38 miles. It is believed to be the steepest route for automobiles in the world. The ascent passes through a number of climatic and vegetation zones. At lower elevations, it is humid and tropical; a little higher up, the terrain becomes subalpine. Here, mamane, a yellow-flowering brush, brightens the slopes, and small birds seem to be everywhere.

Right: Haleakala is sacred to the Hawaiians. The remains of ancient stone structures within the crater indicate that religious ceremonies were held here more than a thousand years ago.

If you are lucky, you might see some of Haleakala's famous honeycreepers. These brightly colored birds are believed to be descended from the first birds (other than sea birds) to have reached Hawaii. Since their arrival, they have evolved into at least 47 species.

From the eastern summit of the crater, the park's other major attraction, the rain-forested Kipahulu Valley, drops thousands of feet in a great sweeping curve down to the coast. The upper valley is a protected wilderness that is home to a profusion of animals and plants as well as an array of insects found nowhere else on earth.

VISITING KIPAHULU VALLEY

The lush Kipahulu Valley begins at a narrow piece of parkland on the southeastern coast of Maui. This coastal area was farmed more than 1,000 years ago, and throughout the valley, you can see archaeological remains of stone walls, temples, and shelters. This is a primal landscape dominated by green forests, meadows, and cascading waterfalls.

The gorge of the 'Ohe'o Gulch cuts through this section of the valley. This defile is filled with picturesque pools, with water cascading from one to the other. Until the 1920s sugarcane was grown along both sides of the 'Ohe'o Stream, and wild cane still grows in patches.

From the gorge, the Pipiwai Stream Trail leads to the lovely Makahiku Falls, which is more than 180 feet high, and then on to a double waterfall. Along the trail you can pick mango and guava fruit.

Higher still, through a luxuriant forest that includes a dense stand of bamboo, which clatters mysteriously in the wind, you arrive at your destination, the Waimoku Falls. Drawing visitors for centuries, this solemn cascade, 300 feet high, fills a jungle clearing with mist and the perpetual sound of falling water.

Right: Silversword grows nowhere else in the world except on this mountain. When the plant matures, after as long as 20 years of growth, it bursts into dazzling, deep-red blooms, then dies.

Opposite: Starting at an elevation of 8,000 feet, the Halemauu Trail descends steeply to the crater floor through a stark but colorful volcanic landscape.

FORMATION OF A PACIFIC VOLCANO

For centuries, Hawaiian legends have explained the way volcanic islands form: Pele, the goddess of fire, moves from place to place around the islands. As she tells others the story of her travels, she stamps her foot, making the earth tremble and forming a new island.

Geologists know that there is some truth to this legend. The spot where an island is likely to appear does move from place to place. Scientists explain this with a theory of "hot spots" and plate tectonics. For some unknown reason, there are approximately 100 hot spots beneath the earth's surface. These places produce more molten rock, or magma, than is produced elsewhere. The Hawaiian hot spot, it turns out, is one of the largest.

The hot spots are stationary, but the dozen or so great plates that make up the crust of the earth are not. The Pacific plate is in constant motion at the rate of about four inches a year. As the plate moves over the Hawaiian hot spot, enough magma rises to create a new island. This young island is pulled away from the hot spot by the movement of the plate, and in time another island forms over the hot spot.

Top: Visitors take a dip in one of the sacred pools of the 'Ohe'o Stream. The waterway cascades through the dense tropical forest of the Kipahulu Valley, much of which has been set aside for scientific research.

Right: Two views of Haleakala (pronounced holly-ah-ka-lah) Volcano. Its name means "House of the Sun," from the legend of the demigod Maui holding the Sun captive inside the volcano's crater.

Left: Thousands of feet below the crater rim, the Pacific Ocean breaks against the dark volcanic headlands and lovely meadows of the park's Kipahulu Coast.

HALEAKALA NATIONAL PARK

Established: 1916; renamed in 1961

Location: Hawaii

When to go: Open all year

Size: 28,655 acres

Terrain: Volcanic mountain and rain forest

Highlights: Haleakala Crater and Kipahulu Valley

Wildlife: Nenes (Hawaiian geese), honeycreepers, parrotbills, and hundreds of other bird species

Activities: Ranger-led walks and talks; hiking, horseback riding, swimming, and back-packing (by permit)

Services: Visitor center, three cabins in the crater, and two campgrounds

Information: Haleakala National Park,
P.O. Box 369,
Makawao, Maui, Hawaii 96768;
808-572-9306

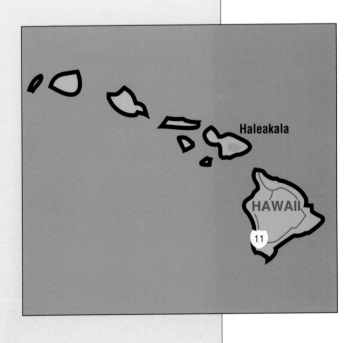

HAWAII VOLCANOES

Fire from Below

The amazing phenomenon featured in this national park begins as a deep rumble, more felt than heard. Sometimes this reverberation is coupled with an ominous, slow hiss that sounds like a disturbed snake. A series of temblors may follow: slow rumbling quakes or great cracking snaps in the ground. These early warnings may last for hours or days.

Suddenly a fissure opens, and as it lengthens rapidly, it emits a blast of steam followed by a fiery fountain of white-hot lava that shoots hundreds of feet into the sky. More and more spouts of lava burst from fresh cracks, and at night they light up the sky for miles around. The frightening roar builds to an overwhelming cascade of sound, and the acrid smell of burning sulfur is everywhere.

It is impossible to witness such a spectacle and not realize that the most colossal raw powers of nature are on display. Scientists who study volcanoes know that there are few better places to see this grandest of all sound-and-light shows than on the Big Island of Hawaii at Hawaii Volcanoes National Park.

There are five volcanoes on the island, two of which are encompassed by the park: Mauna Loa and Kilauea. Both are among the world's most active volcanoes. More than 4,000 feet above sea level and still growing, Kilauea rises from the

Left: The spectacular eruptions of Puu O are rarely dangerous to people. The volcano gives plenty of warning, which scientists can now readily interpret, before it begins spewing lava.

Far Left: A river of lava flows from Kilauea, releasing great billows of steam when it reaches the Pacific Ocean. The volcano has added more than 300 acres to the Big Island of Hawaii.

southeastern flank of the older and much larger Mauna Loa.

These fiery mountains are not huge steep-sided cones topped with snow, like Fuji-san in Japan or Mount Rainier in Washington. Instead, these volcanoes in Hawaii rise more gently from the sea to a great caldera on the summit. This kind of mountain is called a "shield volcano" because the top looks like an ancient warrior's shield lying face down.

Mauna Loa, which means "long mountain," rises 13,677 feet above the Pacific Ocean. It is second in height in Hawaii only to Mauna Kea, a quieter volcano. The visible elevation of Mauna Loa is topped by many mountains, but its actual size is astonishing. Measured from its base, which is 18,000 feet below the surface of the Pacific, Mauna Loa exceeds Mount Everest in height by 2,000 feet. The world's most massive single mountain, its bulk is about 100 times that of Mount Rainier.

Atop Mauna Loa, a large caldera, called Mokuaweoweo, contains several summit craters that have erupted in the past, covering much of the caldera floor with lava twisted into

KILAUEA SUMMIT

Often called the "drive-in volcano" because its summit is so accessible, Kilauea has an awesome caldera two miles across and three miles long that is surrounded by ragged, barren cliffs hundreds of feet high.

Inside this vast bowl, fantastic lava shapes cover miles of barren landscape that looks like a desert on another world. Most of the time, the caldera emits wisps of steam. In its southern end, there is a great fiery pit that is 3,000 feet across and more than 200 feet deep. This volcanic crater is called Halemaumau, or "fern house."

Up until 1924, the crater contained a lake of molten lava that bubbled constantly. More recently, the crater has been the scene of some of nature's most spectacular fireworks, as wild fountains of fire spray upwards, while lava flows from great fissures in the floor. According to legend, this is the home of Pele, the goddess of fire. Geologists confirm that this may be the earth's major opening for the upward flow of lava.

Above: A tender young fern takes root in a type of rough, ropy lava flow known as *pahoehoe*. Such plants are pioneers in the process of re-vegetation that begins after lava has cooled.

HAWAII VOLCANOES NATIONAL PARK

Established: 1916; renamed in 1961

Location: Hawaii

When to go: Open all year

Size: 229,177 acres

Terrain: Volcanic mountains, desert, and forest

Highlight: Kilauea crater

Wildlife: Hundreds of bird species

Activities: Ranger-led, walks, talks, slide shows, and films; hiking, backcountry fishing, art center, workshops, seminars, and backpacking

Services: Visitor center, a museum, three campgrounds, a hotel, and cabins

Information: Hawaii Volcanoes National Park, Hawaii 96718; 808-967-7311

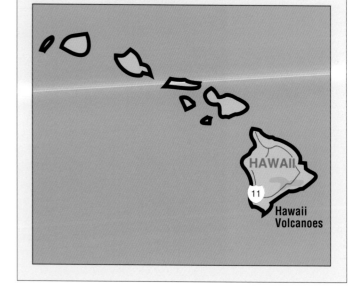

nightmarish shapes, great pits, and cinder cones. Eruptions within the craters of both of the park's volcanoes are relatively harmless. The outbursts give fairly reliable advance notice, and because they are exciting to watch, an impending eruption typically draws thousands of people to the crater's rim.

More dangerous eruptions break out through huge fissures in the flanks of the mountains as underground pressures mount, forcing lava from the openings. Flowing slowly like a great, hot tidal wave down the slopes, an advancing wall of lava can destroy crops and whole villages in its path.

Despite this awesome power for destruction, which is rarely dangerous to human life, Hawaiians have always cherished and respected the awesome mountains. Ever since the first people arrived here about 1,500 years ago in huge double-hulled, ocean-going canoes, Hawaiians have woven fascinating legends about the gods and goddesses who inhabit the volcanoes and cause them to erupt.

Left: This spray of lava looks like fire, but it is not flaming. The orange glow is the lava itself, which has a temperature of around 2,000 degrees Fahrenheit when it comes out of the earth.

HOT SPRINGS

An Unusual City Park

Hot Springs is the smallest of our national parks, and in many ways, it is the most unusual. Instead of covering hundreds of thousands of acres of spectacular scenery and wildlife habitat, Hot Springs is nearly surrounded by a city. And instead of protecting natural resources from commercial interests, Hot Springs National Park continues the commercial use of its major natural resource, a practice that began in the 1800s.

Mineral-rich water comes bubbling forth from the park's 47 natural hot springs at the rate of nearly a million gallons a day. The National Park Service collects, cools, and supplies hot water to commercial bathhouses both inside and outside the park.

The waters of Hot Springs have long been used for medicinal purposes, first by Native Americans, then later by the Spanish explorer Hernando De Soto. He is said to have taken a hot bath here in 1541. The unique properties of the waters were investigated in 1804 under authority of President Thomas Jefferson. In 1832, President Andrew Jackson set aside the springs as a special federal reservation.

The long history of presidential interest and involvement allows park officials to refer to Hot Springs as the "oldest area in the national park system." After all, the government took control of the area 40 years before Yellowstone National Park was created.

Throughout the nineteenth century, the town of Hot Springs prospered as a health spa, with people coming from around the world to "take the waters." Entrepreneurs covered the springs and piped hot water into bathhouses along the

city's main street, Central Avenue, which is also called Bathhouse Row. The elegant bathhouses that line the avenue were modeled after some of the finest spas in Europe.

Today, Central Avenue is the heart of the national park. Hot Springs Mountain, from which the water flows at 143 degrees Fahrenheit, rises above the street. Its lower slopes were once covered by an unusual, white porous rock, called tufa, which was formed of minerals deposited by the hot water. But the slopes were altered more than a century ago when the rock was covered with tons of dirt, and professional landscapers planted shrubs, trees, and grass.

Left: Native Americans called this place, which they considered sacred, the Valley of the Vapors. Even on hot days, the water, which comes out of the earth at 143 degrees Fahrenheit, condenses when it hits the air.

Opposite: When Hernando de Soto visited the Hot Springs area in 1541, the springs in which he and his men bathed would have looked something like the Cascade, which has been restored to its natural state.

167

In recent years medical science has detracted from the mystique of taking hot mineral baths, which in the past were believed to cure or provide relief from such ailments as arthritis, paralysis, and gout.

Today you can still enjoy a hot springwater bath at the Buckstaff, the only bathhouse operating on Bathhouse Row. The Fordyce Bathhouse is a restored spa in which visitors can see stained-glass windows, assorted statuary, and gleaming pipes, as well as the luxurious tubs in which the aficionados of another age undertook three-week therapy courses of daily hot baths and massages.

Opposite:
Fashioned after the palatial spas built in Europe in the nineteenth century, Bathhouse Row is now the centerpiece of Hot Springs National Park.

HOT WATER FROM THE GROUND

There is only one hot spring in its natural condition in Hot Springs National Park. Called the Cascade, it is located approximately a half mile above bathhouse-lined Central Avenue.

The spring was created in 1982 by park officials who cleared away tons of dirt, decaying plants, and other materials that had collected over decades. The water flowing from the Cascade may have fallen as rain as long ago as 4,000 years and then seeped through fractures in the earth's surface. It was heated when it passed over hot, igneous rocks deep within the earth. Eventually the water returns to the surface through faults in the rock of the mountain.

The new tufa rock being created by the Cascade hot spring is building up at the rate of one inch every eight years. The bright blue-green color on the rock is algae, the only plant species that can survive in such hot water. Several concealed natural springs are located along the Tufa Terrace Trail, which is on the opposite side of the Grand Promenade from the Cascade.

HOT SPRINGS NATIONAL PARK

Established: 1921

Location: Arkansas

When to go: Open all year

Size: 5,839 acres

Terrain: Urban area and wooded hills

Highlights: The Cascade and Fordyce Bathhouse

Wildlife: 150 bird species

Activities: Ranger-led walks, bathhouse tours, and campfire programs; hiking, horseback riding, bird-watching, hot baths, whirlpools, steam cabinets, hot packs, and massages

Services: Visitor center, one campground, and six bathing facilities

Information: Hot Springs National Park, P.O. Box 1860, Hot Springs, Arkansas 71902; 501-623-1433

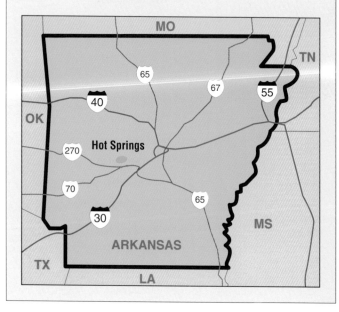

ISLE ROYALE

Island Wilderness

Separated from mainland Michigan, which claims it, by 56 miles of rough water (and from the shores of Minnesota by only 20 miles), Isle Royale is pure wilderness, with no roads and almost no development. The island's isolation has helped to keep it pristine, looking much as it did more than two centuries ago when white men first stepped on its shores.

This is the only place in the United States south of Alaska where wolves roam free and where they still play a useful role in the local ecology by preying on weaker members of other species. Moose, the wolf's main prey, also inhabit the island. While the wolves are elusive, you frequently see moose in the meadows alongside woodland trails.

The 45-mile-long, five-mile-wide island rises out of the vastness of Lake Superior, the largest of the Great Lakes. This unusual national park consists of Isle Royale and another 200 smaller islands that surround it. Although seaplane flights are available from Houghton, Michigan, most visitors reach Isle Royale on boats operated by the Park Service. The ride takes two and a half hours from Grand Portage, Minnesota, or approximately six hours from either Houghton or Copper Harbor, Michigan.

On Isle Royale you are truly in the forest primeval. A long ridge extends along the length

Left: Wary and largely nocturnal, red foxes are seldom seen by hikers. Once hunted for their fur, the animals are now protected within park boundaries.

Far Left: Exposed bedrock at Pickerel Cove was laid bare by receding glaciers, which left a series of parallel ridges across the island. The park contains some of the oldest exposed rock in the country.

of the island; its landscape has been complicated by eons of geological upheaval and sculpting by glaciers. Isle Royale was born as glacial ice withdrew during the last Pleistocene ice age 10,000 years ago. The island's high ridges rose above the great basin that eventually would become Lake Superior, and glacier-scoured gouges in the barren rock became the island's lakes.

Wind and water forged a lovely coastline punctuated by numerous inlets and quiet little coves. Soon the first migrants, including mosses, lichens, and wind- and bird-borne seeds, arrived and found little nooks and crannies in which to begin the arduous work of building soil and vegetation. Humans probably came to Isle Royale about 4,500 years ago. There are more than 1,000 small copper mining pits scattered around the island, some of them dating to around 2500 B.C.

Animals also found their way to the island, and a unique ecosystem began evolving. Moose, the island's largest inhab-itants, are believed to have walked over from the mainland early in this century during a particularly cold winter when lake ice permitted such a passage. Wolves, the island's most famous residents, crossed the ice in the 1940s.

Since the late 1950s, scientists have used the island's isolated ecosystem as a natural laboratory in which to study the relationship between wolf as predator and moose as prey. In recent years, however, the wolf population has dropped significantly, and scientists are not sure why.

Right: A bull moose feeds on aquatic plants. Moose are the primary prey of the island's gray wolves, which keep the moose population in check by culling young, old, or debilitated members of the herd.

Opposite: Boaters can explore some 200 small islands within park boundaries. These are treacherous waters, however. Ten major shipwrecks, some dating to the late 1800s, may be explored by experienced scuba divers.

Above: Richie Lake is one of more than 40 lakes on the island. Most offer excellent fishing. Common species are northern pike, trout, yellow perch, walleye, and a variety of sunfish.

Opposite: Sunset illuminates the deceptively calm surface of Lake Superior. Located approximately 20 miles from the Minnesota coast, Isle Royale is one of the most remote parks in the lower 48 states. It may be reached only by boat or seaplane.

ISLAND WOLVES

Perhaps drawn by a large and growing moose herd, a few wolves crossed ice-covered Lake Superior to Isle Royale in 1949. For two decades the wolves fed on old, young, or weak moose. Both the moose herd and the wolf pack benefited from the relationship. The wolves prevented the moose from overpopulating the island and eating themselves out of house and home. The wolf pack itself leveled out at about 50 members, which was appropriate for the size of the moose herd.

By about 1980 the symbiosis was no longer working. There were fewer moose upon which the wolves could prey, and the wolf population was falling. By 1989 the moose population had again increased, but there were only 11 wolves left. Park biologists are mystified at the continued drop in the number of wolves. One reason for the decline may be that wolves breed slowly: Only the dominant pair of wolves in a pack produces a litter each year.

ISLE ROYALE NATIONAL PARK

Established: 1931

Location: Lake Superior

When to go: June to September (the park is closed November to mid-April)

Size: 571,790 acres

Terrain: Wilderness island, coves, lakes, and valleys

Highlights: Ancient copper mines

Wildlife: Moose, timber wolves, beavers, squirrels, foxes, and birds

Activities: Ranger-led nature and history walks, canoe tours, and lighthouse and copper mine tours; films, boating, canoeing, hiking, scuba diving, fishing, and backpacking

Services: Visitor center, one lodge, and backcountry campsites

Information: Isle Royale National Park, 800 East Lakeshore Drive, Houghton, Michigan 49931; 906-482-0984

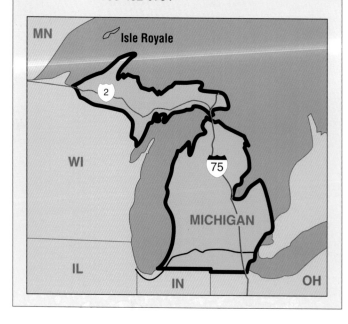

JOSHUA TREE

Oasis in the Desert

When western explorer John C. Fremont encountered a Joshua tree in 1844, he described it as "the most repulsive tree in the vegetable kingdom."

An overstatement? Perhaps. But Fremont's words contain a grain of truth. With its shaggy bark, ungainly limbs, and clusters of daggerlike leaves, the Joshua tree is truly an odd-looking plant.

Of course, this oversized member of the lily family has also had its share of admirers. After struggling across the Mojave Desert in 1849, William Manley called it a "brave little tree to live in such barren country." And a party of Mormon emigrants who passed through in 1851 took courage from the upraised limbs that seemed to beckon them across the desert just as, in biblical times, Joshua called forth the Israelites: "These green trees are lifting their arms to heaven in supplication. We shall call them Joshua trees!"

Opinions about the Joshua tree may vary, but one thing is certain: It is superbly adapted to this harsh desert environment. An average of about four inches of precipitation falls annually in this parched country; temperatures soar to more than 110 degrees in summer and dip well below freezing in winter. Strong winds are common in all seasons.

Like other desert plants, the Joshua tree survives these arid conditions by soaking up moisture during infrequent showers and minimizing evaporation during long periods of drought. Once a year, usually after a heavy spring rain, it sends forth a spectacular, if somewhat bizarre-looking, blossom that resembles an artichoke with creamy yellow petals. Other flowering plants come alive, too, putting on a dazzling display of spring color that includes lupine, blazing star, golden coreopsis, Mojave aster, scarlet locoweed, and desert mallow.

The Joshua tree, of course, is only one element in a complex web of life that makes up the park's fragile desert ecosystem. There are at least three distinct ecological zones within the park. The Joshua tree forest is found in the Mojave

Above: The stony visage of "the Trojan" stares down on hikers on the Hidden Valley Trail. Like other formations in the park, this boulder has been sculpted by wind, water, and ice.

Left: Clear desert light falls across the long, pointy leaves of Mojave yucca and slabs of bare granite. The park's rock formations are popular with climbers.

Right: Although imposing, perhaps even dignified, the Joshua tree is no beauty. "One can scarcely find a term of ugliness that is not apt for this plant," said writer J. Smeaton Chase.

Opposite: Teddybear cholla is typical of the hardy plant life of the lower, drier Colorado Desert in the eastern half of the park. Also known as jumping cholla, it is notorious for pricking unwary passersby.

Desert in the western half of the park. Elevation ranges from about 2,000 to 5,000 feet with a few peaks in the Little San Bernardino Mountains such as Keys View and Eureka Peak exceeding 5,000 feet.

This is also where one finds the jumbled granite formations that have become so popular with rock climbers. Several well-maintained trails lead through boulder fields, canyons, and other geological features in the appropriately named Jumbo Rocks, Wonderland of Rocks, and Hidden Valley areas.

The eastern half of the park is in the Colorado Desert. It is occupied by the low-lying Pinto Basin, surrounded on three sides by the eroded walls of the Eagle, Coxcomb, and Pinto mountains. Vegetation in this region is dominated by the cre-

osote bush and other tough desert plants with occasional patches of spindly ocotillo and spiny cholla cactus. Although hotter and drier than the west side of the park, its plant life is equally, if not more, diverse.

The third ecosystem exists in and around the park's five oases. Shaded by dense stands of fan palms and enlivened by the sound of bird song, the oases are islands of life where green plants flourish and animals such as coyotes and the occasional bighorn sheep come to slake their thirst.

The oases attracted a variety of human inhabitants, too, including the native Serrano and Chemehuevi Indians, who trapped small game in the underbrush and gathered the nutrient-rich seeds of palm trees and mesquite. Later, a steady

JOSHUA TREE WILDLIFE

Observing desert wildlife can be a challenging endeavor. Many animals are nocturnal, coming out of their hiding places only at night to hunt or gather food. Others tend to be shy, skittering away as soon as you approach.

Birds are perhaps the most commonly seen animals here. In addition to species that reside in the desert year-round, there are a variety of birds that migrate through the park in spring and fall or spend the entire winter.

Less visible are the park's many reptiles. Although small lizards are often seen scooting across the rocks, most reptiles—including several species of snakes, some poisonous—are rarely encountered (and many visitors prefer it that way). Occasionally seen is the slow-moving desert tortoise, one of the few threatened or endangered species that reside in the park.

Consider yourself lucky if you spot one of the park's large mammals. Coyotes, perhaps the cleverest critters in the West, are sometimes seen loping across a road or hiking trail. Bighorn sheep keep their distance on the park's rocky slopes. Rarely seen bobcats prowl about in the mornings and evenings. Jackrabbits and a variety of rodents, including ground squirrels, kangaroo rats, and white-footed mice, scamper across the desert floor.

As always, it's wise to shake out boots and sleeping bags in order to remove unwanted guests such as scorpions, which pack a painful, though rarely fatal, sting.

stream of prospectors and teamsters used the oases as way stations in their travels across the desert, and ranchers utilized them to graze and water livestock.

As always in the desert, these precious water sources are the hub of both human and animal activity.

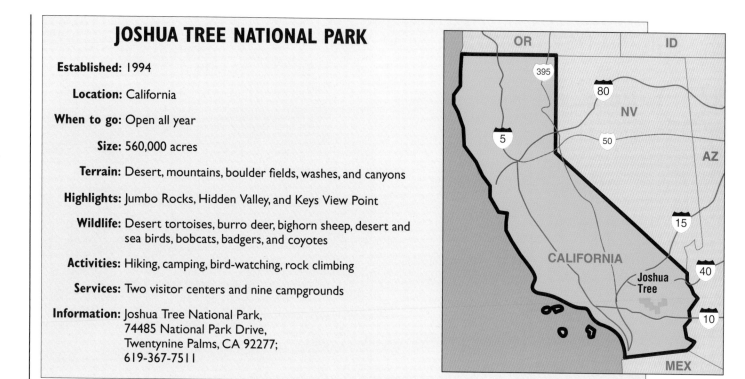

JOSHUA TREE NATIONAL PARK

Established: 1994

Location: California

When to go: Open all year

Size: 560,000 acres

Terrain: Desert, mountains, boulder fields, washes, and canyons

Highlights: Jumbo Rocks, Hidden Valley, and Keys View Point

Wildlife: Desert tortoises, burro deer, bighorn sheep, desert and sea birds, bobcats, badgers, and coyotes

Activities: Hiking, camping, bird-watching, rock climbing

Services: Two visitor centers and nine campgrounds

Information: Joshua Tree National Park,
74485 National Park Drive,
Twentynine Palms, CA 92277;
619-367-7511

Opposite: Huge slabs of granite, assembled by ancient geological forces, resemble manmade sculptures in the ever-changing light of the desert.

Right: A native of the Mojave Desert, the Joshua tree is well-adapted to extreme aridity and a wide range of temperatures. Its thick, fibrous leaves help prevent evaporation, and its shaggy bark protects it from insect invaders.

KATMAI

The Smoking Valley

Streams flowing down from encircling mountains have carved this stark valley, filled with ash and pumice to depths of hundreds of feet, into deep and spectacular gorges. One sheer-walled canyon, hewed by the serpentine Ukak River, is crowned by cliffs 400 feet high. Although a few plants have been able to gain a tenuous foothold here and there, the valley is essentially lifeless, a moonscape of desolation that looks as if it had recently suffered a terrible catastrophe.

The great cataclysm occurred in 1912, when a volcano erupted here on the Alaska peninsula with a force that geologists believe was 10 times greater than the explosion that took the top off Mount St. Helens in 1980. The eruption was heard hundreds of miles away as a new volcano formed and an older one collapsed.

For hundreds of miles up and down the coast, the daylight sky was darkened by thousands of tons of ash thrown more than 30,000 feet into the sky. Global temperatures cooled for weeks, and as far away as Vancouver, British Columbia, acid rain burned up clothing that was hanging outdoors to dry. It is believed that nobody witnessed the actual eruption, because it occurred in a wild and uninhabited region far from towns or villages. But the great event put Katmai on the front pages of America's newspapers, sparking an interest in the region.

In 1916, botanist Robert Griggs led an expedition into the area to find out exactly what had happened. As he climbed up on top of Katmai Pass, he could scarcely believe his eyes: "The whole valley...was full of hundreds, no thousands—literally, tens of thousands—of smokes curling up from its fis-

sured floor." Thus inspired, he named the place the Valley of Ten Thousand Smokes.

Katmai was designated a national monument in 1918. In 1980, Congress enlarged its area and reclassified it as a national park.

Today, the smokes, which were fumaroles that sent jets of steam as high as 1,000 feet in the air, are gone. But the place is nearly as bleak as it was on the day that Griggs first set foot in the valley, now the centerpiece of Katmai National Park. The valley is almost totally barren, crossed only by a few streams. One of several hiking trails leads 3,800 feet up an icy, ashy slope to the rim of Mount Katmai. When you look down into the caldera from here, you can see a lake the color of a robin's egg.

Above: These Alaskan brown bears can afford to wait for an easy catch. Each year more than a million salmon come to the waters of Katmai.

Opposite: Fed by snowmelt, the chilling waters of Margot Creek flow into Naknek Lake, tumbling over 30-foot falls at the foot of Mount Kelez.

Katmai: The Smoking Valley

Below: When Mount Katmai collapsed in on itself during the eruption in 1912, it created the basin for this lake, which was still boiling when botanist Robert Griggs visited the area in 1916.

Another highlight of the park is Novarupta, a 200-foot dome of volcanic rock believed to be the extrusion plug of the 1912 eruption. Geologists believe that most of the lava and ash was emitted here and that magma was drawn away from nearby Mount Katmai, which collapsed as a result.

Beyond the Valley of Ten Thousand Smokes, Katmai is a wilderness wonderland of mountains, rivers, and forested valleys. The park contains 15 active volcanoes, many still emitting steam from open vents and fissures.

The park's other main attraction is North America's largest population of brown bears. Approximately 750 of the protected animals roam through the park's huge backcountry areas. One of the best places to see these magnificent creatures is from a viewing platform overlooking Brooks Falls, a half-mile from the Brooks Camp Visitor Center. Here, nearly every day in spring and summer, travelers from all over the world witness the marvelous spectacle of the great bears skillfully catching fish.

Below: When Mount Katmai collapsed in on itself during the eruption in 1912, it created the basin for this lake, which was still boiling when botanist Robert Griggs visited the area in 1916.

THE BEARS OF KATMAI

Brown bears, North America's largest land carnivores, have made the Katmai area their home since the most recent Pleistocene ice age. Averaging 1,000 pounds in weight and measuring up to 10 feet long, the bears spend the long Alaskan winter in dens they have excavated in hillsides or under exposed tree roots. Not true hibernators, they sleep fitfully off and on, sometimes waking up enough to wander around outside in the snow.

They wake up for good in early spring (April in Katmai), poke their heads outside, and lumber out to find food. If the bear is a female, there is a good chance that she has birthed a pair of cubs during the winter. Visitors to the park delight in the marvelous and often amusing antics of these clumsy youngsters fishing for the first time.

Bear-watching in the park is best in midsummer, the spawning season of sockeye salmon. Sometimes bears dive completely under the water of a fast-moving river to catch fish, while at other times they dexterously catch jumping fish in midair.

KATMAI NATIONAL PARK

Established: 1980

Location: Alaska

When to go: June to mid-September

Size: 4,090,000 acres

Terrain: Forested valleys, streams, mountains, and volcanic terrain

Highlights: Bears at Brooks Falls and the Valley of Ten Thousand Smokes

Wildlife: Brown bears, moose, wolverines, small mammals, and birds

Activities: Ranger-led walks, talks, evening programs, and bus trips to the Valley of Ten Thousand Smokes; bear-watching, hiking, kayaking, canoeing, boating, mountain climbing, aerial sightseeing, fishing, float trips, and backpacking

Services: Visitor center, three lodges, cabins, a wilderness retreat, and a backcountry campground

Information: Katmai National Park,
P.O. Box 7,
King Salmon, Alaska 99613;
907-246-3305

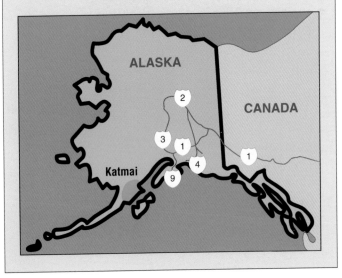

Top: Naknek Lake and the Brooks River are popular fishing spots for both bears and humans. The park's most spectacular wildlife event occurs in summer, when brown bears, some weighing as much as 1,000 pounds, converge here to gorge on spawning salmon.

185

KENAI FJORDS

Mountains and Ice

The Harding Ice Field, occupying nearly 700 square miles and as much as a mile thick, crowns the mountains of Kenai Fjords in south-central Alaska. This is a raw, ragged land that has not yet recovered from the great Pleistocene ice sheets that flowed over most of Alaska 12,000 years ago.

The rocks of the coast here are so jagged, sharp, and uneroded that land and sea seem to be locked in a fearsome struggle for dominance: The sea challenges the land with deep, lovely fjords and hundreds of inlets and coves, while the coast abuts the Gulf of Alaska with great, rocky headlands and clawlike peninsulas.

Kenai Fjords reflects the essence of Alaska's southern coast. The park's dynamic geology includes spectacular mountains with great glaciers flowing down between them to the sea, as well as awesome fjords that provide a habitat for thousands of nesting seabirds and seafaring mammals. The land has a rough, unfinished look to it.

A vast sea of whiteness, the Harding Ice Field feeds more than 30 glaciers that reach out from it, flowing down through the mountains like great tentacles. This glistening field of ice is covered here and there by great dunes of snow that move constantly with the vagaries of the wind. In places, the peaks of mountains buried by the ice since the Pleistocene Era rise above the icy plain. In stormy weather, these peaks, called *nunataks*, seem to float like castles on a sea of white. They are awesome reminders of an age not so long ago, when vast sections of the world were cold, frozen, and lifeless.

Vast as it seems today, the Harding Ice Field is a relatively small remnant of the much larger ice cap that once covered

the entire region. As the ancient ice advanced, then retreated, then advanced again over the centuries, it carved out the rugged coastline of the Kenai Peninsula and gouged out the fjords. Finally, as the earth's climate warmed, the ice began melting, leaving in its wake a spectacular landscape and habitats for throngs of wildlife.

At least 20 species of seabirds nest by the thousands on the rocky crags of the fjords. Clown-faced puffins make their homes among the rocks. These stubby birds with short wings fly only with difficulty, but they are as graceful underwater, when diving for fish, as they are ungainly in the air. Peregrine falcons hunt for small mammals on the rocky islands that dot the coastline, while bald eagles soar among the cliffs of the fjords.

Black bears and wolverines, along with moose and lynx, roam a narrow zone of lush rain forest between the coast and the icy mountainsides, which is home to mountain goats that climb on rocks so exposed they would give pause to an experienced mountaineer.

Above: The icy mass of Holgate Glacier flows into Aialik Bay, one of the park's spectacular fjords. Tour boats are a popular way for visitors to explore the frozen coast.

Opposite: Sea lions—some weighing as much as 2,000 pounds—are often seen resting on rocky islands. The park shelters more than 20 species of marine mammals, including sea otters, harbor seals, dolphins, and whales.

EXPLORING KENAI FJORDS

The inlets, coves, fjords, islands, and even glaciers of Kenai Fjords offer hikers and boaters many opportunities for exploring and seeing wildlife in a spectacular natural setting.

The barren Chiswell Islands, serviced by ferry boat, are an excellent place to see giant Steller sea lions basking, playing, and fighting on the rocks. Females, which give birth to pups in June, may weigh as much as 600 pounds, while the bulls can weigh more than a ton.

McCarty Fjord, in the southern end of the park, slices deeply into the mainland for 23 miles with great cliffs towering nearly a mile above the water. Here and in adjacent Nuka Bay is a fascinating array of terrain, including a 900-foot waterfall and several historic gold-mining camps. Along the shores you are likely to see black bears, moose, martens, and river otters, while in the icy inlets protruding into the landscape you might see a humpback whale jumping almost completely out of the water in a dramatic display of power and joy.

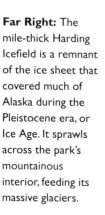

Far Right: The mile-thick Harding Icefield is a remnant of the ice sheet that covered much of Alaska during the Pleistocene era, or Ice Age. It sprawls across the park's mountainous interior, feeding its massive glaciers.

Right: Kenai's long, narrow fjords were carved by glacial ice during the Pleistocene era. Glaciers continue to flow out of the mountains. Some, such as the Holgate, Aialik, and McCarty glaciers, spill into the sea.

KENAI FJORDS NATIONAL PARK

Established: 1980

Location: Alaska

When to go: Open all year (winter access is limited)

Size: 669,540 acres

Terrain: Mountains, glaciers, coast, fjords, and islands

Highlight: Harding Ice Field

Wildlife: Moose, black bears, wolverines, martens, lynx, mountain goats, bald eagles, peregrine falcons, puffins, harbor seals, northern sea lions, sea otters, and humpback whales

Activities: Ranger-led hikes to glaciers and ice field and evening campfire programs; mountain climbing, sailing, camping, fishing, kayaking, aerial sightseeing, boat trips, cross-country skiing, dogsledding, snowshoeing, and backpacking

Services: Visitor Center in Seward, ranger station, two cabins, and one campground

Information: Kenai Fjords National Park,
P.O. Box 1727,
Seward, Alaska 99664;
907-224-3874

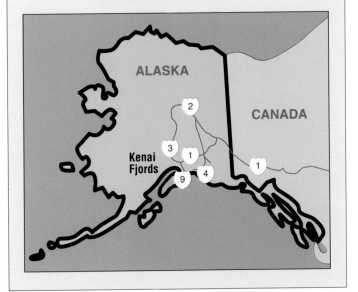

Top: A majestic bald eagle surveys its territory from the limb of a bleached snag. The wingspan of adult birds may exceed seven feet.

Center: A moose cow browses in a verdant mountain meadow. These ungainly animals thrive in and around the park's spruce forest, streams, ponds, and wetlands.

Bottom: Horned puffins rest on a sea stack. Horned and tufted puffins are among the most common sea birds visitors are likely to see on the shore and nearby islands.

KOBUK VALLEY

Land of Shifting Sands

T he Kobuk Valley is pure Arctic terrain. Its wide bowl is filled with great boreal forests and a tundra that creeps up the lower slopes of the mountains.

Flowing from its headwaters in the Brooks Range on the east and draining into the Hotham Inlet, the Kobuk River glides across the heart of the valley. Its floor is so flat that the river drops only about two or three inches every mile. The river's barely detectable current makes it look like a lake in places where it is especially broad.

The river is the main artery for transportation in Kobuk Valley National Park, which lies entirely above the Arctic Circle and has no roads. A paddle or motor trip on the river usually begins from the little settlement of Ambler on the east side of the park and ends in Kiana, a village outside the park's western boundary. Floating on the river, you will find solitude in the wilderness. Kobuk Valley is one of the least visited national parks. In both 1993 and 1994, there were fewer than 3,000 visitors to this remote natural realm where Eskimos still hunt the great herds of caribou that migrate through the area each summer.

Placid and pleasant, the Kobuk River flows through land belonging to the Inupiaq Eskimos. In some places, steep banks rise above the water, while elsewhere great boreal forests line both shores, interrupted by lakes and tundra. In late August and early September, you can sit above the river and watch huge herds of caribou swim across the river, the great antlers of the males bobbing and swaying with the motion of the water. In a stream that meanders through a grassy meadow down to a confluence with the river, you may see a grizzly

bear fishing for dinner, its enormous paws slashing through the water with lightning speed.

South of a bend in the river on the eastern side of the park, great sand dunes appear suddenly. This is an Arctic Sahara in a strange and unlikely setting. East of the dunes is Onion Portage, the park's best known feature, which is named for the wild chives that grow there. For thousands of years, migrating caribou have splashed across the river here on their way south for the winter. Here, too, evidence indicates that hunters have waited for them.

In 1961, at Onion Portage, archaeologist J. Louis Giddings found what has been called the most important archaeological site in the Arctic. Giddings uncovered a two-acre area that yielded evidence of flint-working technology representing seven different cultures dating back at least 10,000 years. The site, now inactive and overgrown, provides important clues about human migration across a land bridge from Asia to North America.

Above: The skulls and antlers of caribou litter the shore of the Kobuk River at Onion Portage. Thousands of animals migrate through the park each year, providing an important source of meat for Inupiaq Eskimo hunters.

Opposite: Cold and slow-moving, the Kobuk River flows across the southern end of the park, skirting the Great Kobuk Sand Dunes, some of which are 100 feet high.

Above: In the Eskimo language, Kobuk means "great river." Ever since people came to live in this place, the Kobuk has been an important source of food, as well as the main east-west travel route.

Opposite: Marsh plants and peat bogs dominate the landscape near the Kobuk River; permafrost prevents drainage, creating a rich environment for moose, waterfowl, and other water-loving creatures.

KOBUK'S MOVING DUNES

Sand is everywhere, shifting and blowing with the wind and the weather. The dunes stretch for 25 square miles south of Alaska's Kobuk River. In this barren landscape, summer temperatures can reach 100 degrees Fahrenheit.

These rolling, active hills, colored yellow and beige, are more than 24,000 years old. Geologists believe they came into existence long before the last ice age, about 10,000 years ago, when the Kobuk Valley was an ice-free refuge with grassy tundra similar to the kind spreading across Siberia today.

The great dunes, along with a smaller five-square-mile tract farther east, were formed by the weathered and wind-blown debris left by an earlier ice age. An unusual combination of geology, topography, and prevailing winds keeps the dunes on the go. Generally inhospitable to vegetation, the dunes of Kobuk Valley are advancing at the rate of about an inch a year through a doomed boreal forest that is in their path. Visitors to the park reach the dunes by boat and can take a short walk through the sand.

KOBUK VALLEY NATIONAL PARK

Established: 1980

Location: Alaska

When to go: Open all year (summer is the most accessible season)

Size: 1,750,421 acres

Terrain: Arctic valley, rivers, lakes, and sand dunes

Highlights: Great Kobuk Sand Dunes and Onion Portage

Wildlife: Caribou, brown bears, small mammals, and birds

Activities: Rafting, kayaking, canoeing, hiking, fishing, aerial sightseeing, and backpacking

Services: Backcountry camping

Information: Kobuk Valley National Park, P.O. Box 1029, Kotzebue, Alaska 99752; 907-442-3890

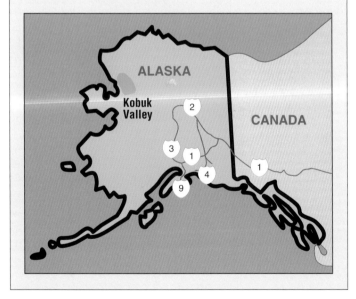

LAKE CLARK

Quintessential Alaska

Excitement for the trip across Cook Inlet from Anchorage to Lake Clark National Park begins even before visitors board their aircraft for the one-hour flight. On some clear days, smoke can be seen billowing in puffs from one or both of the park's two active volcanoes, named Iliamna and Redoubt. More than 10,000 feet high, the volcanoes are only 35 miles apart.

More and more white-mantled mountains loom up as your plane approaches the park. Suddenly you are flying through Lake Clark Pass, and before you spreads out what looks like an endless enchanted wilderness: rugged mountains with gleaming blue glaciers flowing down through the valleys between them, winding rivers, waterfalls cascading hundreds of feet to end in multicolored sprays of foam, and the flanks of mountains covered with blazing red and orange fireweed. As you fly out of the pass, the great lake where you will land appears.

Lake Clark is 50 miles long and five miles wide, and its color is a lovely blue. On its southeastern shore, the little community of Port Alsworth is the site of the park's field headquarters and the place where most visitors settle in for a good, long look at some of North America's most outstanding and varied scenery. All of Alaska seems to converge here.

The backbone of the park is the Chigmit Mountains, a range as rugged as mountains can get; they appear to rise directly from great sheets of ice. These peaks are the spectacular meeting place of the Alaska range that dips down from the north and the Aleutian range that rises up from the south.

To the west is the great Turquoise-Telequana Plateau, a wilderness preserve for herds of wandering caribou. The tun-

dra here is similar to Alaska's North Slope. Black bears wander the mountains, along with Dall sheep, at their southernmost limits here. Alaska's state tree, the Sitka spruce, is at its northernmost limit in the park. Throughout the valleys, there are dense conifer forests.

The park has three rivers—the Mulchatna, Tlikakila, and Chilikadrotna—that have been officially designated "wild and scenic" by the National Park Service. In this strictly fly-in park with no roads, canoeing or kayaking is the only way to get close to this magnificent wilderness. The park's rivers and lakes also offer some of the finest fishing in the world, with Dolly Varden trout, northern pike, and five kinds of salmon (chum, king, coho, humpback, and sockeye).

Connecting the southwestern end of Lake Clark to Iliamna Lake, the Newhalen River is an excellent place to watch the

Above: An unnamed waterfall cascades near the mouth of a mountain cave. Its frigid, glacier-fed water flows toward Little Lake Clark near the mouth of the Tlikakila River.

Opposite: A view of Lake Clark and surrounding mountains from Port Alsworth, the only ranger station in the park. The lake is 50 miles long, five miles wide, and more than 800 feet deep.

annual migration of salmon heading upriver to spawn. This river is as clear as fine crystal, making it possible to see the salmon from an airplane. During the spawning season, which begins in late June, the fish arrive at the Alaska coast after traveling thousands of miles through the Pacific. In peak years the migrating salmon color the river red. As many as nine million fish fight their way upstream to Lake Clark and its shallow tributaries where they themselves were spawned.

EXPLORING LAKE CLARK

Wilderness reigns supreme around Lake Clark. This is a land of glaciers, volcanoes, alpine peaks, and costal inlets with countless seabirds, herds of caribou, and great roving bears.

Lake Clark is a dazzling place to explore. Access to most areas of the park is by water—either air taxi, boat, or kayak. Taking a kayak out on Lake Clark itself is an open invitation to wander where you will, exploring countless inlets and miles of coastline. The smaller lakes in the park also offer excellent kayaking, while some of the rivers give experienced kayakers or rafters fine white-water experiences.

Surprisingly, the opportunities for organized hiking in this great wilderness park are somewhat limited. The only maintained hiking trail is just two miles long. Beginning in Port Alsworth on the shore of Lake Clark, the trail leads through a forest of birch and black spruce, around bogs and ponds, and along the shore of the rough-and-tumbling Tanalian River. You will see moose in the ponds, Arctic grayling fish in the river, Dall sheep on the slopes of Tanalian Mountain, and bears practically everywhere.

Elsewhere in the park, there are good but less well marked hikes around the shores of lakes, between lakes, and into the rugged mountains.

Right: Pulled by gravity and fed by heavy precipitation, glaciers flow between jagged mountain peaks, relentlessly grinding underlying rock into a fine glacial powder.

Opposite: The dense boreal forest of spruce, poplar, birch, and aspen fringe Lake Clark, providing habitat for a variety of creatures, from large predators such as brown bears and wolves to moose, beaver, and other plant-eaters.

LAKE CLARK NATIONAL PARK

Established: 1980

Location: Alaska

When to go: Summer

Size: 4,045,000 acres

Terrain: Mountains, lakes, valleys, coastline, and tundra

Highlights: Lake Clark Pass and salmon migrating on Newhalen River

Wildlife: Moose, black bears, Dall sheep, Arctic graylings, wolverines, small mammals, and dozens of seabirds

Activities: Kayaking, rafting, boating, fishing, backpacking, mountain climbing, bird- and wildlife-watching, aerial sightseeing, and hunting (by permit)

Services: Several small fly-in lodges at western end of park

Information: Lake Clark National Park,
4230 University Drive, Suite 311,
Anchorage, Alaska 99508;
907-271-3751

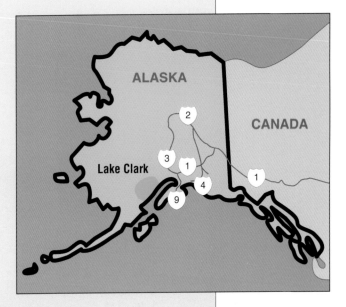

LASSEN VOLCANIC

Land of Scorched Earth

Volcanism displays its spectacular and destructive artistry in this vast panorama of devastated landscape. Lassen Volcanic National Park is evidence of the incredible violence that occurs below the surface of our planet. The last eruptions here took place early in this century, but Lassen still has an otherworldly terrain of broken mountains, scorched land, bubbling mud pots, and hissing steam.

Lassen is at the southern end of the Cascade Mountains, which contain other volcanic peaks, such as Mount Rainier, Mount Shasta, and Mount St. Helens. This national park is a churned-up landscape of stark features that have been given such descriptive names as Chaos Crags and Chaos Jumbles. At one spot, intriguingly called Bumpass Hell, powerful-smelling vapors drift over boiling hot springs with golden flakes floating on their surface. The flakes are crystals of iron pyrite, or fool's gold, that have been carried along by super-heated steam.

Visitors to the park amble through dense sulphur fumes to see thick, gurgling clay, tinted pastel colors with minerals from far below the earth's surface. The centerpiece of the park is Lassen Peak, a volcano that erupted 150 times over a one-year period beginning in 1914. The peak was once part of a much larger volcano called Mount Tehama.

Today, Lassen is a 10,457-foot-high pile of gray volcanic rock that is covered by snow much of the year. The mountain is so barren of life that it has been called a "vertical desert," but watchful hikers on the trail to its summit may very well encounter a ground squirrel or a swarm of tortoiseshell butterflies.

The park is a natural laboratory that spectacularly displays the effects of past volcanic action as well as the ongoing turmoil beneath the earth's surface. Throughout the park, cinder crags and magma canyons offer proof of former violence, while gurgling fumaroles and sulphur fumes suggest the possibility of a fiery future. In one place, appropriately called the Devastated Area, scorched and fallen trees dot the landscape amid such signs of renewal as saplings, grass, and stubborn new bushes.

The Cinder Cone, a nearly cylindrical mountain of lava, rises ominously above the pine forest. The cone formed as it emitted lava and ash that then fell back onto its slopes as multi-colored cinders. The crater at the top of the Cinder Cone dates to its most recent eruption in 1851. That display of natural fireworks was seen more than 100 miles away.

Manzanita Lake also adds to the drama of the park's furious landscape. Geologists believe that the lake was formed

Above: Although the heavily wooded park is within a single day's drive from San Francisco, it remains lightly used by the public.

Opposite: Reflected in the clear water of Manzanita Lake, Lassen Peak's serene looks belie the volcano's recent history of violent eruptions.

when a volcanic dome suddenly collapsed, possibly the result of an earthquake. Riding a gigantic cushion of trapped air, millions of tons of rock and debris flew across about two miles of flat terrain. The horizontal landslide was stopped by a mountain, where it blocked a creek to form the lake.

Right: The 755-foot Cinder Cone last erupted in 1851, creating a symmetrical mound of dark, volcanic cinders. The view from the top takes in surrounding peaks and lakes.

LASSEN PEAK

Battle-scarred Lassen Peak was once part of a much larger mountain that began 200,000 or more years ago as molten rock, called magma, which flowed upwards from the depths of the earth. Slowly, over the years, the magma formed an immense cone 15 miles wide and 11,500 feet high. Eventually the great volcano collapsed, giving birth to smaller mountains around its rim. Lassen Peak is one of these mountains.

In the mid-nineteenth century, when the first settlers came to California, the area around the peak was dotted with bubbling springs and vents spewing steam. But the peak itself appeared calm. The newcomers assumed the volcano was extinct.

In May of 1914, the peak showed signs of life, pouring forth enormous columns of steam and gases from its top. Three scientists decided to climb to the summit to see if they could determine whether the volcano would erupt. As they peered down into a new crater near the top, they felt the ground rumbling beneath them. They turned and fled down the mountain, barely surviving the blast.

Lassen erupted 150 more times during the next year. Finally, in May of 1915, the mountaintop exploded. Lava poured down the slopes, and a blast of ash and gas shot out of the volcano, rising 30,000 feet in the air and devastating a three-square-mile area.

Since then, except for a small eruption in 1921, the volcano has remained dormant. Until Mount St. Helens exploded in 1980, Lassen was the last volcano to erupt in the lower 48 states. Scientists are now studying the devastated landscape around Lassen to see how long it is likely to take for the barren slopes of Mount St. Helens to recover.

A trail leads to the summit of Lassen Peak. From here, there are fine views of the bleak and darkened remains of the 1915 eruption.

Left: Bumpass Hell is a mile-wide valley where thermal activity fills the air with sulfurous steam, and pools can be as hot as 196 degrees Fahrenheit.

LASSEN VOLCANIC NATIONAL PARK

Established: 1916

Location: California

When to go: Open all year (winter access is limited)

Size: 106,372 acres

Terrain: Scoured volcanic landscape, lakes, and mountains

Highlights: Lassen Peak and Cinder Cone

Wildlife: Deer, ground squirrels, small mammals, and birds

Activities: Ranger-led nature walks and talks, children's and evening programs; hiking, swimming, fishing, boating, field seminars, cross-country and downhill skiing, and backpacking

Services: Visitor center, guest ranch, and eight campgrounds

Information: Lassen Volcanic National Park,
P.O. Box 100,
Mineral, California 96063;
916-595-4444

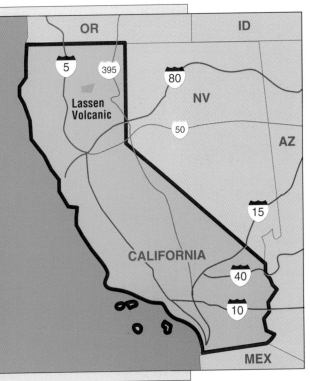

201

RAINBOW DOME
CEILING 45 FT.

MAMMOTH CAVE

Passages Beneath the Earth

Beneath the forest-covered hills of southern Kentucky, you will discover the world's largest system of caves. There are about 330 miles of underground passages—on five different levels—that have been explored or mapped so far.

This cave is so vast and startling, its scores of passageways, rooms, and pits so rich in history, that it has been designated a United Nations World Heritage Site. The full extent of Mammoth Cave is still unknown. New caves and passageways are almost constantly being discovered, as the underground frontiers of this spectacular labyrinth extend deeper and deeper into a netherworld that almost defies belief.

People have been crawling through and living in the cave since prehistoric times. Anthropologists believe that Native Americans first discovered the great cave about 4,000 years ago. To light their way in the intense underground darkness, they fashioned torches from bundles of cane like that which still grows nearby. Charred remnants of these ancient torches have been found miles inside the cave in chambers lined with thousands upon thousands of gypsum crystals in myriad shapes. Apparently, these crystals were highly valued by the early spelunkers.

The cave also holds ancient footprints, undisturbed for centuries, as well as bits of clothing and abandoned sandals. Two miles from the cave entrance, the mummified body of a gypsum miner who died some 2,400 years ago has been discovered. He was crushed to death by a five-ton boulder. The man's body and his clothing are perfectly preserved.

Mammoth Cave was first discovered by white pioneers in the 1790s, and guides have been leading astonished tourists

through it ever since. During the War of 1812, the cave was mined near its entrance. Slaves did most of the work, filling large leaching vats with dirt and rock from the cave. The nitrate crystals produced by this operation were used to make gunpowder.

Nearby, in a section of the cave reached by a spectacular underground passage called Broadway, there is a spot called Methodist Church, where religious services are believed to have been conducted in the early 1800s. Visitors to this area today are treated to an experience much like that of earlier tourists. Cave guides turn off the lights and throw torches through the immense underground chamber, allowing visitors to see with their own eyes the way the cave looked before electric lights were installed.

Booth's Amphitheater is an underground room once visited by Shakespearean actor Edwin Booth, the brother of Lincoln's assassin, John Wilkes Booth. Edwin Booth is said to have re-

Left: The well-preserved remains of Lost John, a mummified Indian, were found by guides under a giant limestone boulder. He was apparently killed in the cave some 2,000 years ago while collecting gypsum.

Opposite: The cave's unearthly formations, such as the stalactites at Rainbow Dome, are created by dripping water laden with calcium carbonate. Traces of iron and manganese add streaks of red and black.

Visitors to the national park rarely see more than the 12 miles of passages that have been opened for tours. But professional spelunkers are still exploring the cave system, drawing new maps and charts, and opening up additional passageways, many of them little more than crawl spaces. In 1972, a long-sought passageway was found that linked Mammoth Cave with the Flint Ridge cave system through Hanson's Lost River, an underground stream. Mammoth Cave has other subterranean waterways: Lake Lethe, the River Styx, and Echo River.

MAMMOTH GEOLOGY

The underground wonderland of spectacular Mammoth Cave was formed, and is still being formed, as limestone, also called calcium carbonate, dissolves in water seeping through the ground.

This phenomenon is usually found where caves occur. Underneath the topsoil on the hills of southern Kentucky, there are two layers of stone. The upper is a sandstone cap that is 50 feet thick in some places. Like an umbrella, it covers the lower layer, a series of limestone ridges.

At places called sinkholes, surface water is able to penetrate the upper sandstone umbrella. As the water works its way downward, the limestone is eroded, forming the honeycomb of underground passageways, amphitheaters, and rooms that make up Mammoth Cave.

Many of the cave's internal features, such as stalagmites, stalactites, and columns, were formed this way. These formations build at the rate of about one cubic inch every two centuries.

Above: The parkland is perforated with craggy sinkholes that mark places where the cave ceiling has collapsed. Water collects in the holes, where it nourishes the rapid growth of a luxuriant variety of plants and trees.

cited Hamlet's "To be or not to be" soliloquy here. Today, a tape recorder eerily resonates these famous words through the cavern.

Nearby is a hole in the ground known as the Bottomless Pit. It was named by early guides, who apparently were not able to see all the way down to the pit's bottom with the weak light of their flickering lard-oil lamps. The "bottomless hole" is actually 150 feet deep.

One of the earliest guides, Stephen Bishop, aptly described the cave as "grand, gloomy, and peculiar." He was a slave of the man who bought the cave in the 1830s, hoping to develop it as a major tourist attraction. Bishop explored and mapped many of the cave's rooms and passages. His assessment of the cave is almost as accurate today as it was 160 years ago. Park officials still do not overlight the cave's interior, guaranteeing that visitors never lose the feeling that they are deep within the earth.

MAMMOTH CAVE NATIONAL PARK

Established: 1941

Location: Kentucky

When to go: Open all year

Size: 52,707 acres

Terrain: Extensive underground cave system and rolling countryside

Highlights: Echo River and Bottomless Pit

Wildlife: Cave-dwelling fish, reptiles, and insects

Activities: Ranger-led cave tours, nature walks, and children's exploration program; fishing, horseback riding, Green River boat trips, bicycling, and backpacking

Services: Visitor center, three campgrounds, and a park hotel

Information: Mammoth Cave National Park, Mammoth Cave, Kentucky 42259; 502-758-2328

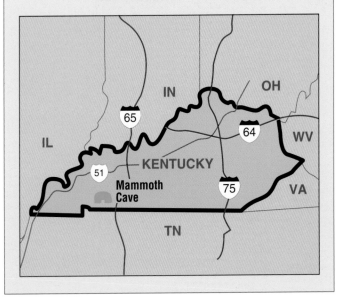

EXPLORING MAMMOTH CAVE

Several tours led by rangers take visitors through different sections of Mammoth Cave's subterranean wonderland. The half-day tour is the most popular. Tour members enter the cave through the Carmichael Entrance that leads down to Cleaveland Avenue. This is a long tubular chamber carved out by underground water. Its walls glisten with white gypsum that has crystallized below the limestone surface. The tour passes through the Snowball Dining Room, where the group may stop for lunch. Afterward, the tour leads through Boone Avenue, a subterranean river chasm so narrow you can reach out and touch both walls. The tour ends at Frozen Niagara, a cataract of flowstone created as mineral-rich water seeps through the walls.

A less arduous walk follows the quarter-mile Travertine Tour. The Wild Cave Tour covers five miles, often by belly crawl, in six hours.

Below: With more than 340 miles of mapped passageways, Mammoth Cave is the longest cave system in the world. Some explorers believe that much of the cave has yet to be discovered.

205

MESA VERDE

Palaces of Stone

Ghosts haunt the cliffs and adobe dwellings of Mesa Verde. The "Ancient Ones" are long gone, but you can feel their spirits as you walk through these silent buildings that have stood for centuries in rock alcoves far above the ground. The structures are startlingly intact, as if they are waiting for the return of their builders, who left suddenly about 700 years ago.

Archaeologists have determined that the people who abandoned these buildings were not the first to live in the region. Nearly 2,500 years ago, nomadic hunters and gathers wandered into what is now the southwestern corner of Colorado. There, in the canyons and gullies of a high mesa, they established what was to become an advanced culture that prospered for more than a millennium.

The first people of Mesa Verde—or green mesa, as it was called by Spanish explorers and priests who came through the area in the sixteenth century—lived in caves. Later they dug pit houses into the ground and covered them with logs and mud. These were farmers who grew corn and beans, and they became basket weavers of consummate skill.

By about the eighth century A.D., they were building houses above ground with poles and mud. These apartment buildings, or pueblos,

were built on the mesa's top and had as many as 50 rooms, usually arranged in the shape of a crescent. By now, the people had given up baskets and begun making pottery, some of which still survives. Decorated with black and white geometric designs, these pots are remarkable for their artistic expression.

Around A.D. 1200, the mesa people moved down into recesses in the cliffs that formed the walls of canyons cut into the mesa. The reasons for the move are unknown today, but archaeol-

Left: Perched high on the cliffs of Soda Canyon, Balcony House was well-protected from intruders. Visitors must climb a 32-foot ladder to enter the ruins and crawl through a narrow tunnel to leave.

Far Left: Tucked into a protective canyon alcove, Cliff Palace is the largest cliff dwelling in the United States, with 23 kivas and more than 200 rooms.

ogists speculate that the people may have been threatened by tribes of newcomers. There, they built sturdy, compact apartment buildings with as many as four stories and 50 rooms. Many of the buildings had courtyards with kivas dug into them. These underground chambers, which are reminiscent of their ancestors' first dwellings on the mesa's top, were used for religious ceremonies.

Although their culture was surprisingly advanced, with complex trade networks supplying such goods as turquoise and shells from as far away as the Pacific Coast, life was harsh for the people of the cliff dwellings, and few lived beyond the age of 35.

In the thirteenth century, the cliff-dwelling people began to leave their homes. By the end of the century, all of them were gone, never to return. Why did they go? Archaeologists once thought they were overtaken by enemies, but there is no evidence of warfare.

Today, many believe that the Anasazis' farming methods may have been so productive that the population grew too swiftly, reaching as many as 5,000 people on Mesa Verde alone. Gradually, this huge population would have taken its toll on the environment. Game would have been hunted out, the soil would have become depleted, and the surrounding woodlands would have been cut away. Years of drought and poor crops would have been the final blow.

Two cowboys discovered the ruins in 1888. Tracking wandering cattle through a snowstorm on top of the mesa, they stopped on the edge of a steep canyon. Through the snow they could see the faint outline of the walls and towers of what looked like a huge palace of stone on the far side of the canyon.

Excited about their discovery, they made a ladder and climbed down to the deserted cliff city, exploring its ghostly network of deserted rooms, where they found such artifacts as tools and pottery. Their condition was so good that some of the items were still usable. They named the dwelling Cliff

Right: A ladder leans against the expertly crafted masonry walls of Far View ruins, originally built in the 13th century and partially reconstructed by archaeologists in 1916.

Mesa Verde: Palaces of Stone

Palace, and archaeologists later determined that no one had stood in the rooms explored by the cowboys for nearly six centuries.

Today, Mesa Verde National Park encompasses more than 4,000 prehistoric sites that were used by the people the Navajo call the Anasazi, which means something approximating "Ancient Ones." The structures and ruins include mesa-top pit houses and pueblos, as well as the ghostly multistoried cliff villages for which the park is famous.

Because of the dry climate, the cliff dwellings are very well preserved. They are located in sandstone canyons that slice the mesa into narrow tablelands. The Anasazi built these dwellings in natural alcoves formed by water that had percolated down through the sandstone. When seeping water reached a denser layer of shale, it flowed horizontally through the canyon wall, eroding the cliff into deep, rounded shelters.

Several of the major cliff ruins are open to visitors, who reach them by trails, walkways, and steps that lead down from the mesa top. The silent stone and the mystery of the Anasazi create an experience most people never forget. Novelist Willa Cather experienced the ruins as "more like sculpture than anything else."

Below: Spruce Tree House is the best preserved and one of the largest cliff dwellings, with 114 rooms and eight kivas. Its high walls still touch the roof of the cave.

EXPLORING SPRUCE TREE HOUSE

Spruce Tree House, Mesa Verde's best preserved ruin, is a fine example of Anasazi construction techniques and skillful stonework. You can reach the site by a short paved trail that crosses the canyon floor through a stand of Gambel oak trees, from which the Anasazi harvested nuts.

Believed to have housed more than 100 people, Spruce Tree House is about 200 feet long and contains eight kivas, three of which have reconstructed roofs. You can climb into one of the kivas through a smoke hole to get a sense of what the dark chamber might have been like during an ancient religious ritual. The dwelling was named by early explorers, who climbed down a tall tree—which they mistakenly thought was a spruce—to reach it.

Other equally remarkable and ghostly cliff dwellings in the park include Cliff Palace, the largest pre-Columbian dwelling in North America, and Balcony House. Perched high up in a cliff alcove, Balcony House was easily defended. Visitors to this site face the adventure of climbing up a 32-foot ladder and crawling through a tunnel on their hands and knees.

Left: Long House, a fortress on Wetherill Mesa, rivals Cliff House in its scope and grandeur. It was opened to park visitors in 1972 after very extensive archaeological study.

MESA VERDE NATIONAL PARK

Established: 1906

Location: Colorado

When to go: Open all year (winter access is limited)

Size: 52,085 acres

Terrain: Mesa, canyons, and gullies

Highlights: Spruce Tree House and Cliff Palace

Wildlife: Rabbits, mule deer, lizards, small mammals, and birds

Activities: Ranger-led archaeological walks, cliff dwellings tours, and campfire programs; way-side exhibits, self-guided tours, limited hiking on two trails (backpacking is not permitted in park), cross-country skiing, and snowshoeing

Services: Visitor center, museum, park lodge, and one campground

Information: Mesa Verde National Park,
Colorado 81330;
303-529-4465

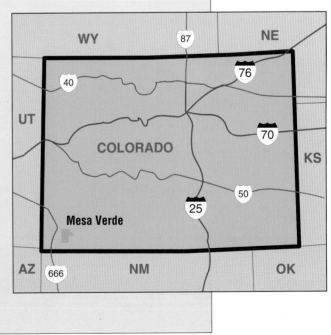

211

MOUNT RAINIER

Icy Heights

Weather permitting, you can see the snow-capped summit of Mount Rainier from more than 100 miles away. It is one of the world's largest volcanoes, and at nearly three miles in height, it also has the distinction of being the tallest peak in the Cascades.

Rainier simply overwhelms the surrounding 6,000-foot mountains, which look like courtiers paying homage to a monarch. The mountain often seems to float alone among the clouds, and when you see it from a great distance, its enormous height, compared with the neighboring peaks, makes it appear closer than it is. In the evenings, as the sun begins dropping below the Pacific horizon, the last light bathes the great mountain's summit, washing it in a warm, pink glow that lasts long after darkness has come to the lowlands.

Even though the mountain is obviously its most important feature, Mount Rainier National Park has many other attractions. Below the great snow fields and glaciers on the upper flanks of Mount Rainier are spectacular fields of wildflowers that burst into bloom in late spring and summer. As the snow melts, an astonishing array of color marches up the slopes. Here, you will see a profusion of monkeyflowers, buttercups, avalanche lilies, Indian paintbrush, asters, and lupines, rushing to bloom during the brief respite from the cold that often ends during the final week of August.

Where there are not meadows, there are great forests, some with trees that are more than 1,000 years old. The woods provide a home for countless birds and animals, such as tiny chickadees, lumbering black bears, and curious, golden-mantled ground squirrels that look like chipmunks without their

stripes. Higher up on the slopes, mountain goats forage for food on ridges blown free of snow. Here too, finches nest in the rocks in summer and feed on heather buds and high-altitude insects, while hoary marmots and tiny pikas hoard dried grass for winter food.

Mount Rainier was forged by fire and shaped by ice. Most geologists believe its birth occurred less than a million years ago on a mass of solidified lava left by earlier volcanoes. New upswellings of lava, ash, and pumice (lava formed with trapped bubbles of gas) poured from the young volcano's vent

Left: Fed primarily by snowmelt, the Muddy Fork of the Cowlitz River knifes through sheer-walled Box Canyon. In places, the gorge is more than 100 feet deep.

Opposite: From late July through August, lupines, monkeyflowers, asters, meadow parsley, Sitka valerian, and other wildflowers offer a lush contrast to snowy mountain peaks.

Below: Bathed in the pastel shades of evening light, Mount Rainier rises more than 14,410 feet into the heavens.

thousands of times. Gradually, layer upon layer of debris piled up, forming a summit cone about 16,000 feet high. Scientists used to think that about 1,500 feet was missing from the top of the peak because it had been destroyed in a great eruption. But today they believe the missing summit was lost in a huge mud flow that took place about 5,000 years ago.

Even without its original top, Mount Rainier is one of America's great peaks and the dominant volcano of the Cascade range. When naturalist John Muir wrote about the mountain, he stated what many people who have seen it feel: "Of all the fire mountains which, like beacons, once blazed along the Pacific Coast, Mount Rainier is the noblest."

CLIMBING RAINIER

More than 10 percent of the surface of Mount Rainier National Park is permanently covered by ice. Even as eruption after volcanic eruption built the mountain, glaciers from the Pleistocene ice ages were carving valleys and canyons on the mountain's slopes.

Today, 25 major glaciers remain. This is the largest collection of permanent ice on a single mountain in the United States south of Alaska. Emmons Glacier is at a lower elevation than any other glacier in the nation.

Austere and serene, the summit of Mount Rainier draws mountain climbers of every age and ability from around the globe. The ascent takes two days, with most of the first day taken up by a long hike through the forests and rocky slopes of the mountain's lower two-thirds.

The second-day trip to the top crosses the weathered surface of a moving glacier, one of six that drops down from the summit. Using ice axes, crampons, and steel spikes fixed to their boots, climbers make their way between deep crevasses that have fragmented the ice into fissures and canyons. In some places they cross crevasses on bridges of unmelted snow.

At the top of the mountain is a small crater left by the most recent eruption a little more than a century ago. Climbers usually walk around it to the Columbia Crest. At 14,410 feet, this is the highest point on the peak; on clear days you have an unsurpassed view of the Pacific Northwest.

MOUNT RAINIER NATIONAL PARK

Established: 1899

Location: Washington

When to go: Open all year (winter access is limited)

Size: 235,612 acres

Terrain: Volcanic peak, foothills, valleys, and canyons

Highlight: Emmons Glacier

Wildlife: Black bears, deer, mountain goats, marmots, pikas, small mammals, and birds

Activities: Ranger-led nature and history walks, hikes, campfire and children's programs, talks, and films; mountain climbing, hiking, fishing, cross-country skiing, snowshoeing, and backpacking (by permit)

Services: Three visitor centers, a hiker information center, two park inns, and five campgrounds

Information: Mount Rainier National Park, Tahoma Woods, Star Route, Ashford, Washington 98304; 206-569-2211

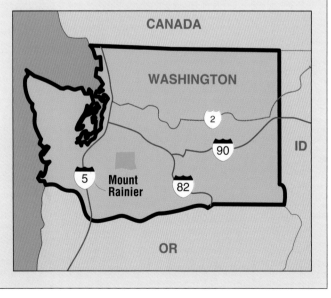

Left: Hikers enjoy excellent views of Nisqually Glacier on a high-country trail in the Paradise area. One of 27 glaciers on Rainier, Nisqually may flow as much as one foot per day in summer.

215

NORTH CASCADES

Alpine Wonderland

This is a land of mountains and ice. More than 300 glaciers are concentrated in Washington's North Cascades National Park—many more than can be found anywhere else in the United States south of Alaska.

The looming presence of mountains also defines this park. Here you will find soaring, glacier-scoured peaks, spires that pierce the clouds, ragged ridges, alpine tarns, and flower-bedazzled meadows in cirques below the mountain summits. On the flanks of the mountains, forests of fir and pine surround tranquil lakes and deep glacial valleys.

North Cascades is also a land of special sounds. On warm days, you can hear the booming crack of sloughing ice and the thunderous roar of avalanches. When the weather is bad, thunder blasts up the valleys and circles around the peaks, while the wind rushes between the mountains and ridges, and down the slopes of glaciers. And always, in this mountain range that was named for its innumerable cascading waterfalls, there is the sound of falling water.

The peaks of the North Cascades are so ragged and vertical that these mountains are sometimes called the American Alps. Like the European Alps, they attract scores of mountaineers, hikers, and backpackers. In 1814, trapper Alexander Ross wrote of this rugged terrain: "A more difficult route to travel never fell to man's lot." The names of some of the mountains in the region attest to the hardships they imposed on early trappers and prospectors: Damnation Peak, Mount Despair, Mount Fury, Forbidden Peak, and Desolation Peak.

North Cascades is a topographic jumble, consisting of two national park units (North and South), as well as two national

recreation areas (Ross Lake, named for the early trapper, and Lake Chelan). All four are administered by the National Park Service. A road through the Ross Lake area, which was completed in 1972, divides the North and South units and makes the alpine wonderland of the park readily accessible.

The mountains themselves create another kind of division within the park. Moist prevailing winds blow in from Puget

Left: Cascading water and fine mists transform bare rocks into a glistening work of art.

Opposite: Mount Sefrit seems to hover above grassy meadows and conifers around Highwood Lake. "Nowhere do the mountain masses and peaks present such strange, fantastic, dauntless, and startling outlines as here," declared Henry Custer after surveying the region in the mid-19th century.

Sound and the Strait of Juan de Fuca. Flowing up the western slopes and cooling as they rise, the moist winds condense into rain and snow. The west side of the park is covered by lush green forests of Douglas fir, western red cedar, and hemlock, which grow to towering heights because the trees receive more than 100 inches of precipitation a year.

By contrast, the western slope of the mountains, lying in the rain shadow of the great peaks, receives on average only a little more than 30 inches of precipitation a year. Douglas firs on the west side of the mountains reach only half the height of firs on the eastern slope. Moisture-loving hemlocks do not grow here at all; instead the western slopes foster trees that tolerate dryness, such as ponderosa and other pine trees.

STEHEKIN VALLEY

Stehekin Valley is a glacial-carved defile of magical scenery in the south end of North Cascades National Park. It has been a mecca for visitors seeking a mountain hideaway since the turn of the century.

The little community of Stehekin lies on the shore of Lake Chelan, which extends south for 55 miles and in some places is 1,500 feet deep. The town of Stehekin was staked out by nineteenth-century prospectors, and its one-room school house was used until 1988.

The valley offers a fascinating look into the history of the North Cascades. The Buckner Homestead gives visitors a sense of the hardships as well as the joys of life on the frontier. Elsewhere there are several mines that can still be explored. Gold, silver, and copper drew hordes of prospectors to this area more than a century ago.

One of the valley's most unusual options is wilderness camping without backpacking: Shuttle buses take campers to one of several backcountry areas where overnight camping is permitted.

Right: With an elevation above 9,000 feet, the ice-clad summit of Mount Shuksan and neighboring peaks prevent moisture-laden clouds from passing over, casting a large rain shadow over the western slope of the Cascades.

CASCADE PASS

There is only one paved road that runs all the way through the park, the North Cascades Highway. As the road climbs higher and higher, the landscape changes from alder forests to huge groves of towering Douglas firs, then to forests of pine, larch, and hemlock, and finally, flowering alpine meadows and a high windy pass. From this point, hikers can set off on an old trail to 5,384-foot Cascade Pass atop a ridge covered with alpine meadows.

In the high meadows, black-tailed and mule deer graze; black bears look for huckleberries, which they rake into their mouths, vine and all, with their claws; and stout marmots sunbathe on rocks. Some lucky visitors catch a glimpse of mountain goats clambering on high rocky crags. They rely on soft cupped pads on their hoofs to give them their incredible traction. Throughout the park roam bobcats, which you will seldom see, and secretive mountain lions. Sleek and tawny, these big cats prey on deer and other mammals, helping to keep the wildlife population in balance.

NORTH CASCADES NATIONAL PARK

Established: 1968

Location: Washington

When to go: Open all year (winter access is limited)

Size: 684,243 acres

Terrain: Rugged mountains, valleys, and lakes

Highlights: Stehekin Valley and Cascade Pass

Wildlife: Black bears, mule and black-tailed deer, mountain lions, bobcats, marmots, pikas, small mammals, and birds

Activities: Ranger-led nature walks, talks, and campfire programs; hiking, boating, fishing, hunting (in season, by special permit), horseback riding, rafting, cross-country skiing, and backpacking (by permit)

Services: Two visitor centers, an information center, a ranger station, two lodges, and seven campgrounds

Information: North Cascades National Park,
2105 Highway 20,
Sedro Woolley, Washington 98284;
206-856-5700

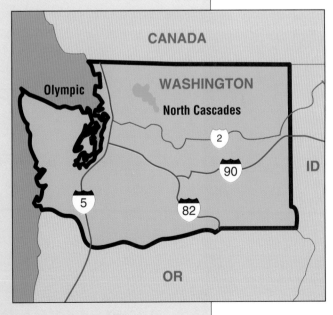

OLYMPIC

Three Parks in One

Come to Olympic, and you enter an enchanted forest, a luminous world suffused with a soft green light reflected and refracted by trees garlanded with club moss and lush growths of ferns and oxalis.

Here, in Washington's Hoh Rain Forest, western hemlock, Sitka spruce, and western red cedars, some with diameters of 25 feet, tower 300 feet above you. These ancient giants, standing on enormous roots called stilts, form great colonnades with inviting, winding side aisles that look like green tunnels leading to another world.

A jumble of undergrowth spreads out far below the forest canopy in the national park on the Olympic Peninsula, located in the extreme northwest corner of Washington. Seedlings that would have been unable to compete with other plants on the forest floor sprout exuberantly on fallen trees, called nurse logs.

From these rotting logs, some saplings may grow into the world's largest specimens of Douglas fir and Western hemlock. The undergrowth is luxuriant and abundant, but it is not impenetrable because its growth is kept in check by the foraging of the park's most famous inhabitant, the Roosevelt elk.

Olympic is the most diverse national park. Along with the Hoh and two other rain forests,

Left: Spruce trees in the park's coastal Kalaloch area exhibit large "potbelly" burls. Racoons, black bears and other forest creatures occasionally visit here looking for a meal.

Far Left: The park protects 57 miles of Washington's wild coast. Battered by the Pacific, the rocky shore, tiny islets, and sea stacks provide a rich habitat for a variety of sea birds and marine mammals.

the park contains two more equally distinct ecosystems: a rugged wilderness seacoast, with stunning headlands and lovely beaches covered with driftwood, and the Olympic Mountains, a rugged range of high alpine meadows, great jagged ridges, and glaciers.

Because of this remarkably diverse landscape, climatic changes within the park are unbelievably abrupt. The western side of the park has the wettest weather in the United States, averaging nearly 12 feet of precipitation each year. The eastern side of the park, which lies in the rain shadow of the mountains, is the driest area on the Pacific Coast north of Los Angeles.

In 1788, an English sea captain named John Mears sighted the peninsula's tallest mountain, which at 7,965 feet is not an extremely high peak, but it rises so dramatically above the sea that it looks enormous. Mears was so overwhelmed by the

LIFE OF THE RAIN FOREST

Olympic's three rain forests, with trees and vegetation as lush as an Amazon jungle, may be the strangest and most fascinating sections of this unusual park.

The richness of these forests exists only because certain conditions are met: Moisture must be incredibly plentiful, and even when it is not raining, the air needs to be humid and misty. And the temperature must be mild, neither too hot nor too cold.

The proximity of the Pacific Ocean helps fulfill these requirements for the Olympic forests. The steep rise of the inland mountains forces Pacific storm clouds to ascend and release their moisture as heavy rainfall. This moisture is then concentrated in long river valleys, which also extend moderate, sea-level temperatures deep inland.

This unique combination of weather and topographical conditions perpetuates the life cycle of these forests. After a tree falls, it can become a nurse log for new seedlings. Bacteria and fungi slowly break down the fibers of the fallen log, which becomes covered by mosses and lichens. This surface is rich in nutrients and allows seeds to germinate and sprout. After a seedling takes root, a young sapling grows. Over time the nurse log rots completely away, leaving a tree standing tall on its stiltlike roots.

Right: Only the muted sound of almost-perpetual rainfall disrupts the peaceful quiet of the Hoh Rain Forest, where soft mosses, gentle ferns, and giant trees create a silent world.

sight that he named the peak Mount Olympus in honor of the home of the Greek gods.

In the 1890s, local residents tried to block a proposal for federal protection of thousands of acres of timber that would restrict the area's huge logging industry. But since 1897 the territory has been under the jurisdiction of either the Department of Interior or the Department of Agriculture. For 24 years it was Mount Olympus National Monument, but the name was changed when the national park was established in 1938.

The heart of the park is the Olympic mountains, a wilderness range that is nearly circular. The mountains are penetrated by 13 rivers that radiate out from their center like the spokes of a wheel. The highlands are up-and-down country, where the peaks and ridges are separated by deep valleys and canyons cut by the rivers. Geologists believe that the rock of the mountains developed beneath the sea because marine fossils are found near the summits.

Around 30 million years ago, the great plate carrying the floor of the Pacific Ocean collided with the North American plate. The upper levels of the seabed plate rose up and crumpled into the Olympic Mountains. Later, glaciers, wind, and water shaped the mountains into what we see today: breathtaking vistas of deep canyons, towering mountain ridges, and meadows dense with wildflowers.

Right: An early snowfall cloaks the jagged profile of Hurricane Ridge, which, at an elevation of more than 6,400 feet, is the highest point visitors can reach by car.

OLYMPIC NATIONAL PARK

Established: 1938

Location: Washington

When to go: Open all year

Size: 922,651 acres

Terrain: Coastal wilderness, rain forest, and mountains

Highlights: Hoh Rain Forest and Mount Olympus

Wildlife: Roosevelt elk, snowshoe hares, Douglas squirrels, Olympic marmots, pocket gophers, small mammals, and hundreds of species of birds

Activities: Ranger-led walks and campfire programs; hiking, boating, fishing, climbing, swimming, windsurfing, waterskiing, river rafting, cross-country and downhill skiing, and backpacking (by permit)

Services: Two visitor centers, a museum, information stations, five lodges, and 15 campgrounds

Information: Olympic National Park, 600 E. Park Avenue, Port Angeles, Washington 98362; 206-452-4501

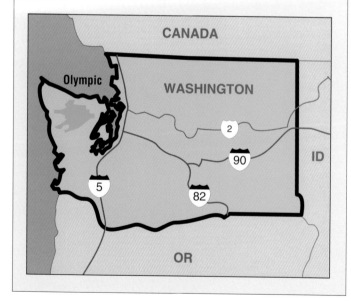

Left: Campers make a temporary home at the edge of a glacial lake with Mount Mystery rising behind them. Wildflowers begin popping up in alpine meadows even before snow has completely melted.

PETRIFIED FOREST

Trees of Stone

In eastern Arizona, a mysterious stretch of bleached badlands is scorched by the blistering sun. This twisted landscape of tortured contours has been eaten away by endless erosion. The forces of nature have carved a high plateau into a jumble of buttes, mesas, gullies, and cones, all tilted at unlikely angles.

Vegetation has been reduced to a few bent plants, such as junipers, low-lying shrubs, shortgrass, and cacti. In spring, enormous fields of wildflowers provide a brief respite from the usual barrenness. This landscape seems to have survived from the beginning of time, but perhaps it is a vestige of the end of time.

Adding another dimension to the mystery of this other worldly scene, great hulking logs of stone cluster here and there on the ground. Many of the logs are broken into segments so perfectly cut that they look like cordwood felled by a prehistoric giant.

The history of this area goes back more than 200 million years. Scientists believe that, eons ago, great herds of dinosaurs roamed through forests of tall conifers, while nearby rivers teemed with armor-scaled fish. The great columns of petrified wood scattered across the desert date from around that time.

Nature produced the mineralized wood under very special circumstances. The trees were uprooted by great floods or perhaps flows of lava, then washed down from the highlands and buried by silt and volcanic ash. Water seeping through the wood replaced decaying organic material cell by cell with multicolored silica. Eventually, the land where the great logs were buried was lifted up by geological upheaval, and wind

and rain began to wear away the overlying sediments, finally exposing the long-buried, now petrified wood.

Each piece of wood is unique, burning with the colors of the Painted Desert, of which Petrified Forest National Park is a part. Some of the great trunks still bear the annual rings that reveal their life histories in prehistoric times. The Paiute believed that the petrified logs were the great arrow shafts of their thunder god, Shinauv. The Navajo said they were the bones of a mythological giant, called Yietso.

After American explorers found these great "stone trees" in the mid-nineteenth century, a steady stream of visitors began making the trek to Petrified Forest. A military survey party passed through the region in 1851, and its members filled their saddlebags with pieces of the petrified wood.

Above: Balanced on the rim of Blue Mesa, this petrified log points to an area in the Painted Desert where trees that lived 200 million years ago were buried.

Opposite: This area of the park has long been known as the Jasper Forest, but most of the petrified trees found here actually were carried here by a river.

227

By about 1870, great quantities of glistening rock were being carried off by souvenir hunters and commercial developers, who cut slabs from the logs for tabletops and mantles. Petrified wood was also blasted apart in search of valuable amethysts or quartz crystals that some of the wood contains. A mill was built to grind the great logs into abrasives. Concerned citizens went to the Arizona Territorial Legislature to seek federal protection for the area, and Petrified Forest was declared a national monument in 1906.

The southern section of the park contains one of the world's largest concentrations of petrified wood. Here, great logs of jasper and agate are interspersed with smaller pieces and fragments glistening in the sun like immense jewels. The northern part of the park encompasses the colorful mesas and buttes of the Painted Desert. Here, sun, sand, and rock create a dazzling range of color and pattern.

Opposite: The eroded sides of beautiful Blue Mesa clearly reveal the layers of sediment in the ancient marsh that buried and transformed the petrified logs.

THE WOODS TIME FORGOT

The Petrified Forest is more than large mineralized trees. It opens a window on an environment that is more than 200 million years old.

Visitors who walk one of the park's hiking trails get a real sense of this forgotten age. Here, it is easy to imagine a marshy wetland where leather-winged pterosaurs soared above rivers filled with giant amphibians, and dinosaurs foraged for food on the banks.

Giant Logs Trail leads to the park's largest fossil log, whimsically called Old Faithful. This great multicolored trunk is 170 feet long, with a diameter of nearly 10 feet. Long Logs Trail, another walking loop, goes to the park's largest concentration of petrified logs. Some of the logs are more than 150 feet long; all are piled in a great logjam.

Other trails lead deeper into the park, giving visitors an even firmer grasp of the past.

PETRIFIED FOREST NATIONAL PARK

Established: 1962

Location: Arizona

When to go: Open all year

Size: 93,533 acres

Terrain: Desert and badlands

Highlights: Old Faithful and the Painted Desert

Wildlife: Kangaroo and pack rats, turkey vultures, coyotes, canyon mice, and rattlesnakes

Activities: Ranger-led nature talks, interpretive exhibits, self-guided auto tours, horseback riding, hiking, and backpacking

Services: Two visitor centers, a museum, and food service

Information: Petrified Forest National Park, P.O. Box 2217, Petrified Forest, Arizona 86028; 602-524-6228

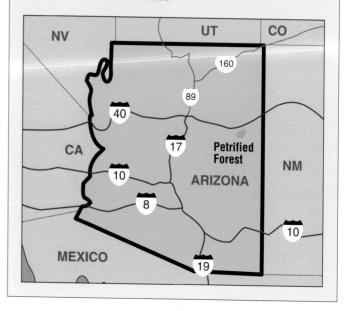

REDWOOD

Land of Tall Trees

This is a magnificent forest of startlingly immense proportion. Full-grown adults look like miniature toy figures next to these great trees that soar 30 stories into the sky, higher than any other living things on earth.

To put their height in perspective, the redwoods are taller than the torch of the Statue of Liberty. The first branches of these trees begin 100 to 200 feet above the spongy, forest floor. They form a delicate green canopy that seems to push the blue sky even higher than it usually seems in the West. California's mighty redwood trees, many now living in their second millennia, are the last large stands of these monumental conifers that flourished all across North America during the lush, humid period before the last ice age.

Here, near the Pacific Ocean, the gentle climate still sustains them. The mighty trees grow in dense groves in a fog belt along the coast, especially in the canyons and river valleys that open directly to the ocean.

Scientists have only recently begun to understand the complex ecosystem of these ancient redwood forests. The branches that form the canopy at the top of the redwoods eventually fall to earth, where they mix with leaves and branches from hemlock and other species and eventually decay. This process sustains a rich web of life. The trees on which some animals depend in turn depend upon other species of animals.

For example, a species of vole eats the fruiting bodies of fungi on dead logs, then excretes the spores on new sites. The spores grow new fungi that are necessary to carry nutrients and moisture to seedlings and tree roots. Owls, flying squir-

Left: Sustained by a gentle, moist climate, coastal redwood trees can reach a height of 30 stories or more—higher than New York's Statue of Liberty.

Opposite: A young maple competes for sunlight with a much taller grove of coast redwoods, some of which exceed 300 feet in height. Ferns, rhododendrons, azaleas, salal, and other shrubs and flowers form a lush understory.

rels, pileated woodpeckers, and martens nest in dead trees and find food throughout the forest.

In the late-nineteenth and early-twentieth centuries, loggers pushed westward across the continent, cutting down mile after mile of the nation's primeval forests. Today, almost all of the old-growth forests are gone. The ancient tress that remain are found along the Pacific, where only about one-fifth of the original 15 million acres of trees that once blanketed the region still stand. Unfortunately for these stately giants, the demand for lumber from redwoods has always been great because the wood resists shrinkage, rot, and decay.

At the beginning of the century, a league to save the redwoods was formed. Aided by the state, the league was able to acquire hundreds of stands and include them in 26 state parks. When Redwood National Park was created in 1968, it incorporated three of these parks, Jedediah Smith, Del Norte Coast, and Prairie Creek, totalling 58,000 acres.

In 1978, Congress added an additional 48,000 acres to the original acreage, including 36,000 acres that already had been logged. One park official described this area as looking like an "active war zone." Today, the clear-cut area is being reclaimed for redwood trees. Officials estimate that it will take 50 years for the logging scars to disappear and another 250 years for the new redwoods to grow to modest size.

Opposite: Sunlight pierces a curtain of mist in the redwood forest. Called "the king of its race" by John Muir, the coast redwood, *Sequoia sempervirens*, survives only along a narrow strip of the northern California coast.

TALL TREES GROVE

Tall Trees Grove, the centerpiece of Redwood National Park, is part of a stupendous stretch of unusually tall redwoods that is called the Emerald Mile. Here, under a vaulted green canopy, sunshine reaches the forest floor only in splintered shafts of light, creating an effect that resembles a gothic cathedral, where great columns of stone are punctuated by stained glass. The mystery of this magical place is further heightened when fog rolls in from the nearby ocean, wrapping the great trees in a wispy gauze of vapor.

Among the giants in Tall Trees Grove stands the world's tallest known tree, appropriately called the Tall Tree. Its top rises almost 368 feet above the ground; its circumference is 44 feet. Foresters estimate that the tree is about 600 years old. This remarkable tree was not measured until 1963, when it was discovered, along with the second and third tallest trees, which stand nearby.

REDWOOD NATIONAL PARK

Established: 1968

Location: California

When to go: Open all year

Size: 110,232 acres

Terrain: Rolling redwood forests and coastal plain

Highlight: Tall Trees Grove

Wildlife: Elk, deer, rabbits, owls, martens, and woodpeckers

Activities: Ranger-led tide-pool and seashore walks, and evening programs; hiking, canoeing, guided kayak trips, horseback riding, fishing, swimming, whale watching, and backpacking

Services: Visitor center, information center, and four campgrounds

Information: Redwood National Park, 1111 Second Street, Crescent City, California 95531; 707-464-6101

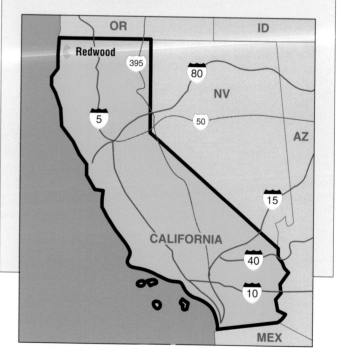

ROCKY MOUNTAIN

Atop the Mighty Divide

This is high country, with sweeping vistas of a jagged skyline crowned by towering summits. Snow lingers here year-round, and the highest cirques preserve remnants of glaciers left over from the last ice age.

In Rocky Mountain National Park, there are 78 peaks that are more than 12,000 feet high; 20 of them reach above 13,000 feet. Contrasting with this jagged terrain, meadows come alive in spring and summer as wildflowers poke their way through the tundra. This park makes accessible a vast wonderland of alpine terrain, towering peaks, high mountain tarns, and glacial moraines.

"Of all the large and rugged mountain ranges in the world, these are the most friendly, the most hospitable," wrote pioneer naturalist Enos Mills, who was instrumental in the creation of Rocky Mountain National Park in 1915. In the southern Rockies, the summers are fairly long, the valleys are broad and inviting, and the mountains are crisscrossed by trails and roads left by miners a century ago, which makes these mountains more affable than other American ranges.

With the highest average elevation of any national park, including those in Alaska, Rocky Mountain sits atop the Continental Divide, the great ridge of mountains that cuts the conti-

nental United States in two. Water on the east side of the divide flows to the Atlantic Ocean, and water on the west side ultimately makes its way to the Pacific.

Much of the parkland is above the timberline, which is about 11,500 feet high in this section of the Rockies. The park's centerpiece, Trail Ridge Road, is the nation's highest paved highway and leads into the heart of a spectacular alpine world. One stunning 10-mile stretch of the road follows a ridge as it rises to 12,183 feet.

In many ways, the timberline, which is so evident from this dramatic drive, is a biological

Above: Elk, or *wapiti*, find cover in the woods during the day, but venture into the open to graze in the evening. Few sounds are as haunting as the bugle of a bull elk during the yearly rut.

Left: It is difficult to imagine a more perfectly appropriate name for Dream Lake, which sparkles at the foot of towering Hallet Peak.

CLIMBING LONGS PEAK

Rising 14,255 feet, Longs Peak, a steep-sided mountain with a flat top, dominates the Front Range of the Colorado Rockies for almost 100 miles. Along with Pike's Peak to the south, it is one of the landmark peaks of the range and one of America's most distinctive mountains.

Some of the most difficult climbing routes in North America lead up the peak's eastern face, a 90-degree cliff that is more than 2,500-feet high. There are also walking routes to the summit.

The most popular of these is the East Longs Peak Trail, which begins at the Longs Peak ranger station. The eight-mile trail climbs nearly 5,000 feet, or almost a mile up. At first it passes through a forest of windblown limber pines, then across a rugged boulder field above the timberline where the real work begins.

After scrambling through a notch called the Keyhole, hikers traverse a rock field then head up a steep granite slab, called the Homestretch, which leads to the summit. The top, which is five acres across, is surprisingly level. From here, on a clear day, the views of the peaks of Rocky Mountain National Park and the mountains beyond seem endless.

Far Right: Often damned by beavers, the park's many streams sustain muskrats, waterfowl, river otters, and moose, as well as dense stands of willow, cottonwood, and conifers.

Right: Like most lakes in the Rockies, Bear Lake is a brillant blue tarn that was scooped out by glaciers during the last ice age.

battle line. Just below the timberline, such hearty trees as sub-alpine firs, limber pines, and Engelmann spruce struggle upwards root by root to find room in which to grow and survive. Above the last trees, an even harsher world challenges the survival of the most robust plants, which cling tenuously to life during a brief growing season and in the face of constant winds. Here are lovely meadows bathed in green grasses and awash with dozens of species of wildflowers that grow low to the ground for protection in this harsh environment.

The park is not just a land of tundra, high rocky places, and ceaseless wind. Below the timberline, you will find lovely hidden places, such as the sublimely beautiful Dream Lake, a rock-rimmed mountain pond nestled in a meadow at the foot of rugged 12,713-foot Hallet Peak.

Countless numbers of wild creatures wander through the woods and meadows. Mule deer and black bears are common sights, and beavers build their dams in many of the streams that drain the lake.

Higher up are elk, while higher still, on seemingly impossible vertical cliffs where they are safe from predators are the elusive Rocky Mountain bighorn sheep, the enduring symbol of this magnificent alpine park.

Right: A mantle of newfallen snow blankets an alpine forest. Storm clouds blowing in from the west are stalled by the Rockies, causing much more precipitation to fall on the western slope than the eastern.

Opposite: The Fall River courses down the east slope of the Rockies near Aspenglen Campground. The park's mountain streams are inhabited by a variety of fish, including the endangered greenback cutthroat and introduced species such as rainbow and brook trout.

ROCKY MOUNTAIN NATIONAL PARK

Established: 1915

Location: Colorado

When to go: Open all year (winter access is limited)

Size: 265,727 acres

Terrain: Alpine peaks and valleys

Highlights: Dream Lake, Trail Ridge Road, and Longs Peak

Wildlife: Bears, Rocky Mountain bighorn sheep, mule deer, elk, beavers, marmots, and cougars

Activities: Ranger-led nature and history walks, campfire talks, and snowshoe walks; hiking, horseback trail rides, bicycling, fishing, rock and mountain climbing, cross-country and downhill skiing, snowshoeing, snowmobiling, and backpacking

Services: Three visitor centers, museum, and five campgrounds

Information: Rocky Mountain National Park, Estes Park, Colorado 80517; 303-586-2371

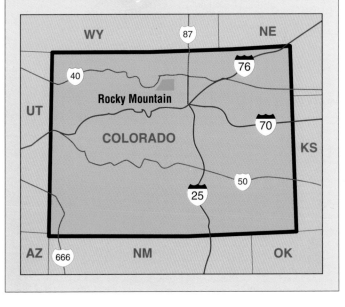

SAGUARO NATIONAL PARK

Sentinels of Sonora

Saguaro National Park takes its name from the saguaro cactus, the giant, many-armed symbol of southern Arizona's Sonoran Desert. Standing as high as 50 feet and weighing as much as seven or eight tons, these silent, slow-growing sentinels are a vital link in the ecology of one of the richest and most varied deserts in the world.

The park is divided into two units on either side of the city of Tucson: Saguaro East sprawls across 67,293 acres, including much of the rocky Rincon Mountains, which peak at an elevation of 8,666 feet. Saguaro West takes in 24,034 acres and is bordered on the south by the lower, gentler Tucson Mountains. Adjoining portions of Coronado National Forest and Tucson Mountain County Park extend the protected area to more than 200,000 acres.

Scenic drives and a network of trails at both units are designed to acquaint visitors with the park's varied geology and wildlife, ranging from the pine forests atop the 8,000-foot Rincon Mountains to the classic desert scenes of cactus and creosote bush at lower elevations. Special attention is paid to the saguaro forest itself, which tends to be concentrated on the rocky slopes, or *bajadas*, at the base of desert mountains.

With only about 12 inches of rain per year and high temperatures in the 100s, survival in the

Sonoran Desert requires special adaptations to heat and drought.

The saguaro, for example, has a long network of roots that grow close to the surface and soak up moisture during brief, infrequent showers. Water is stored in the saguaro's gelatinous tissue which, when fully expanded, can hold as much as 200 gallons. Thick, waxy skin minimizes evaporation, as does the absence of leaves. The plant's notorious spines repel thirsty animals, provide shade, trap cool air, and protect it from drying winds.

Many animals avoid the intense heat by hunting or gathering food only at night or, like the roadrunner and Gila monster, during the cool hours of dawn and dusk. Birds such as the Gila woodpecker and gilded flicker make holes in the saguaro itself, using the burrows as protection against both searing heat and biting winter cold. When the original occupants move out of the holes, any of several other bird species move

Above: Saguaros blossom in the spring. Colorful flowers open after sunset every evening, only to wilt the next day. Bees and other insects feast on the flower's nectar, as do longnose bats, white-winged doves, and other animals.

Far Left: Although dominated by towering saguaros, the Sonoran Desert is home to a variety of vegetation, including hedgehog and prickly-pear cactus, spindly ocotillo, ubiquitous creosote bushes, and the notoriously prickly cholla cactus.

in, including cactus wrens, American kestrels, screech owls, and western kingbirds.

The jackrabbit employs quite a different method to stay cool. It uses its prominent ears as radiators, ridding itself of excess heat directly through the skin. Perhaps the most intriguing adaptation is that of the kangaroo rat, which is able to survive a drought by drawing all the water it requires from seeds.

Humans have also learned to survive in the Sonoran's harsh climate. Native Tohono O'odham Indians—descendants of the ancient Hohokam Indians whose archaeological remains are scattered throughout the desert—still harvest the succulent fruit of the saguaro for a variety of foods such as jam, syrup, and ceremonial wine. They also utilize the seeds of the saguaro and, after the cactus dies, the strong woody skeleton that holds it erect.

Casual visitors should note that the best time for hiking is early morning or evening, when the sun is low on the horizon and shy desert animals such as coyotes, javelinas, and seldom-seen bobcats are busy looking for food.

Above: Saguaro National Monument was set aside in 1933 to protect a forest of mature saguaros. It was expanded several times and redesignated a national park in 1994.

CLIMATE AND LIFE ZONES

First-time visitors often expect the desert to be unrelentingly hot. But the weather at Saguaro National Park is actually quite variable. While daytime temperatures in summer regularly soar above 100 degrees, nights can be as much as 20 degrees cooler.

Temperatures sink well below freezing in winter, and snow is not uncommon, especially at the higher elevations. Perhaps the best time to visit is from late fall to early spring, when daytime temperatures hover around the 60s and 70s.

Climate varies significantly by elevation, too, tending to become cooler and wetter the higher one climbs. By hiking up the Rincon Mountains, for example, one passes through several distinct plant communities, rising from the low desert scrub inhabited by the saguaro forest to the mid-range oak and pine woodland. At the highest elevations, there are stands of ponderosa pine and Douglas fir that are similar to the forests of the northern United States.

Left: Giant saguaros are silhouetted by the warm glow of sunset, when the desert's many nocturnal creatures emerge from their hiding places to search for food.

SAGUARO NATIONAL PARK

Established: 1994

Location: Arizona

When to go: Open all year

Size: 91,000 acres

Terrain: Desert, mountains, and cactus and pine forests

Highlights: Valley View Overlook, Cactus Forest Drive, and Desert Ecology Trail

Wildlife: Desert birds, jackrabbits, coyotes, and bobcats

Activities: Self-driving tours, hiking, and camping

Services: Two visitor centers and six backcountry camping areas

Information: Saguaro National Park,
3693 South Old Spanish Trail,
Tucson, AZ 85730-5699;
520-733-5153 (east visitor center) or
520-733-5158 (west visitor center)

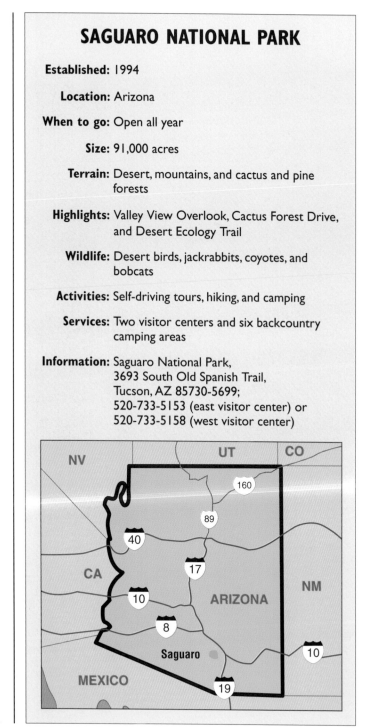

Right: Hohokam Indians inhabited the northern Sonoran Desert for hundreds of years before disappearing in the fifteenth century. Archaeological remains, such as this intriguing petroglyph at Signal Hill, have been found throughout the park.

SEQUOIA-KINGS CANYON

High Mountains, Big Trees

Suppose national parks had themes. The theme of these two adjacent California parks, administered jointly since 1943, would probably involve the three impressive superlatives to which they lay claim.

The combined parkland contains the planet's largest living things, giant sequoia trees that are so huge they far surpass the size of any other species. It's also the site of Mount Whitney, at 14,495 feet the highest mountain in the lower 48 states. Here, too, is Kings Canyon, the deepest in North America, plunging down steep granite walls more than 8,000 feet from its rim to the Kings River below; making it more than half again as deep as the Grand Canyon.

Sequoia is America's second national park. It was established in 1890 as a wilderness sanctuary to protect groves of giant sequoia trees that were being destroyed by logging. Kings Canyon, a steep-walled valley, was mandated as a national park in 1940, absorbing General Grant National Park, which had been created by Congress almost as an afterthought just three weeks after it approved neighboring Sequoia.

The two parks encompass most of California's High Sierra country. They contain thousands of acres of sequoias and some of the nation's wildest and loveliest alpine scenery. Here are miles of sweeping mountain vistas, range

after range of snow-capped peaks, high meadows, rocky ridges, and green forests of pine and ponderosa.

The largest trees by weight and volume in the world, the sequoias in this park are the last relics of a species that covered much of the world before the most recent ice age. The glaciers swept over all but a few thousand acres too high in the Sierra Nevada for the ice to reach, destroying all the trees in their path.

Left: The celebrated General Grant Tree, second largest in the world, is more than 267 feet tall and 107 feet around; it's been called the nation's Christmas tree.

Far Left: The sound of flowing water is one of the recurring themes of the parks. Swollen by melting snow, long stretches of white water thunder through glacier-carved canyons.

Sequoia-Kings Canyon: High Mountains, Big Trees

Sequoias used to be considered a subspecies of the coastal redwoods that are found in Redwood National Park and elsewhere. The scientific term for the redwood tree is *Sequoia sempervirens*—a name that came from Sequoyah, the inventor of the Cherokee alphabet, who was much admired by the Austrian botanist who named the redwoods. The same name was at first also given to the giant trees of the Sierra Nevada. Today, botanists realize the Sierra Nevada sequoia is a separate species. They now call it *Sequoia gigantea*.

The groves of these huge trees seem to go on forever, but these sequoia forests cannot compare with what existed here just a little over a century ago. Logging of what was then one of the world's finest and most extensive old-growth forests began in about 1862 and continued relentlessly until the turn of the century. Vast stands of these giant trees were wiped out, including at least two trees, and possibly as many as four, that were bigger than the biggest tree in the world today, the park's famed General Sherman sequoia. Two of these trees

were cut for a reason that today seems frivolous. Their trunks were put on display at world's fairs.

In the park, you can still see the Centennial Stump, the remains of a gigantic sequoia cut down for exhibition at the 1875 Centennial in Philadelphia. Nearby is the Big Stump Trail, a one-mile path that leads through an incredible wasteland of downed logs, stumps, and fallen trees, sad reminders of an earlier era when these giants were only valued for their wood.

The bigness of the park that is evident in these great trees is also reflected in its spectacular alpine backcountry. This park is almost completely wilderness. Its boundaries encompass most of the Sierra Nevada. These mountains are the longest and highest unbroken range in North America, stretching more than 400 miles from north to south.

A jagged, sawtooth chain of rocky ridges punctuated by sheer granite peaks, the section of the Sierra Nevada within Sequoia and Kings Canyon is not a range of individual moun-

Below: *Sequoiadendron giganteum*, commonly known as giant sequoias, are the largest living things on the planet. The last of their kind, they were stranded in the Sierra Nevada by a climatic change thousands of years ago.

Sequoia-Kings Canyon: High Mountains, Big Trees

tains but a great upheaval of solid granite. Its western side rises somewhat gradually from foothills to more than 13,000 feet, then plummets dramatically down its eastern flank to Owens Valley.

Several major rivers rise within the drainage basins of these mountains, which contain country so remote that a backcountry hiker may not see another person for days at a time. There is one spot in the park that is said to be more distant from a road than any other location in the lower 48 states.

John Muir Trail runs through the park. This high-mountain walking route took 40 years to construct. From Yosemite National Park it leads south for 218 miles across the snow-swept top of the High Sierra all the way to the flank of Mount Whitney.

Dozens of supplementary trails connect with the Muir trail, giving hikers good access to the park's stunning alpine world of knife-edge ridges, glaciers, high mountain tarns, and meadows filled with wildflowers.

Right: A steep stairway climbs to the top of 6,725-foot Moro Rock, where visitors are treated to this view of the Great Western Divide.

Opposite: The General Sherman Sequoia, the world's largest tree, is mostly trunk. Its lower limbs all died because the immense tree prevented them from getting enough sunlight.

THE GENERAL SHERMAN TREE

The statistics of the General Sherman sequoia, the biggest living thing on earth, are staggering. Its bulk, estimated at four and a half million pounds, far exceeds any other tree on earth. Its 275-foot height, although not as tall as some redwood trees, is certainly respectable. Its lowest branch is 130 feet above the ground, which is high enough that a 12-story building would not reach it. This branch, incidentally, is itself larger than any tree in the United States east of the Mississippi River.

The General may be as old as 2,500 years, and it is still growing. Botanists believe that the tree adds enough wood each year to build another 60-foot-tall tree. The total lumber contained within the General's huge bulk would build more than 50 three-bedroom houses. Among the last of their species, thousands of giant sequoias still remain in the park. Fortunately, they are reproducing themselves in logged-out areas at a rate that insures their survival for centuries if we continue to protect them.

Some of the stumps cut during the nineteenth century show rings dating back 3,000 or more years. Experts believe it is likely that some of the trees now standing were alive during the Bronze Age, 3,500 to 4,000 years ago.

The longevity of the sequoia is due to several factors. For one thing, its bark, which can be two feet thick, is unusually resistant to fire, insects, lightning, and disease. The trees also are exceedingly vigorous, outgrowing and dominating other species in the forest. Their only known weakness is a shallow root system that occasionally allows them to topple over without warning in a mild breeze.

GENERAL SHERMAN

KING OF CANYONS

The Kings Canyon area was first proposed as a national park by John Muir as early as 1891, the year after the creation of Sequoia National Park, but the park was not fully established until 1940. It bears the name of the river that in 1805 a Spanish explorer dubbed Rio de los Santos Reyes, or "river of the holy kings."

Formation of this stunning steep-walled cleft in the granite of the Sierra Nevada began about 25 million years ago as powerful geologic forces lifted up the land in what is now eastern California. About three million years ago, the highest peaks towered three miles above sea level. Then a series of earthquakes along fault lines in the earth deep below the Sierra Nevada cracked off the mountains' eastern face, which began sliding downward. This accounts for the stunning appearance of the eastern side of the mountains, which rises dramatically from Owens Valley.

Swiftly moving rivers made faster by gravity began carving narrow V-shaped canyons through the mountains. Over eons, the canyons plunged deeper into the earth. During the Pleistocene ice ages, glaciers advanced into the Sierra Nevada and began scooping out basins that eventually became lakes, at the same time gouging out the walls of these canyons, making them sheer and steep.

Nearly one and a half miles deep, Kings Canyon is the most dramatic of these glacier-carved defiles. Several other canyons in the park exceed 3,000 feet in depth, and Kern Canyon is nearly 6,000 feet deep.

Opposite: Shaded by a dense stand of vegetation, the Kings River churns below the weathered granite cliffs of the Sentinel at the base of Kings Canyon.

SEQUOIA-KINGS CANYON NATIONAL PARKS

Established: 1890, 1940; Joint administration, 1943

Location: California

When to go: Open all year (winter access is limited)

Size: 864,383 acres

Terrain: Mountains, alpine valleys, canyons, and forests

Highlights: General Sherman sequoia and Kings Canyon

Wildlife: Bears, deer, bobcats, weasels, pine martens, wolverines, coyotes, and mountain lions

Activities: Ranger-led talks, walks, and children's programs; fishing, bicycling, horseback trail rides, pack trips, downhill and cross-country skiing, and backpacking

Services: Three visitor centers, a nature center, four lodges, and 14 campgrounds

Information: Sequoia-Kings Canyon National Parks, Three Rivers, California 93271; 209-565-3341

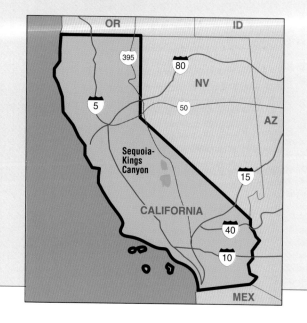

SHENANDOAH

The Mighty Blue Ridge

There rises a great ridge in western Virginia, where the gentle hills and valleys of the Piedmont begin to give way to green mountain heights. Even from a distance of many miles, it looks like an impenetrable barrier to the land that lies behind it.

For many years the so-called Blue Ridge was an insurmountable obstacle to our nation's westward expansion. Its mild eastern flank sloped down to the agricultural heartland of Virginia and farther east to the burgeoning towns and cities along the Atlantic coast. Pioneers who wanted to go west from here thought twice about the ruggedness of the ridge, its height, and the fact that there were no low-lying passes through it. But the pioneers and adventurers who made it to the top of the ridge were greeted by a spectacular sight: the lovely Shenandoah Valley. This green paradise of endless forests and meadows cut by winding rivers and streams was so inviting that the valley itself seemed to hold all the promise of the West.

Shenandoah contains more artifacts of human history than most other national parks. It lies along a spectacular but populated section of the Blue Ridge that nearly cuts Virginia in two. Unlike most national parks, it is a place where people have lived for many generations. The section of the great ridge encompassed by the park is crossed by few passes, and the imposing mountain range forced early pioneers through the Cumberland Gap and into broad Shenandoah Valley.

To make this area suitable for a national park, which was mandated by Congress in 1926, the Commonwealth of Virginia acquired nearly 4,000 privately owned tracts of land in

the Blue Ridge Mountains and Shenandoah Valley. The state then donated the land to the nation. No other park required the acquisition of so much private land, or required the National Park Service to create a park out of land that had been so widely inhabited by people.

At the time it was established, much of the future parkland consisted of eroded hillsides, worn farmland, and thin second- or third-growth forests. Timber had been harvested from these woods since the early-eighteenth century. By 1935, when the park was opened to the public, nearly 2,500 mountain people had moved from their cabins and farmhouses and resettled outside the park's borders at government expense. A few mountain people continued to live in the park even after it opened, but they are all gone now.

The long, narrow park follows the Blue Ridge from the southwest to the northeast. Today, the forests are returning;

Above: Congress made Shenandoah a national park in 1926. At the time, the only other national park east of the Mississippi was Acadia in Maine.

Opposite: Craggy rock outcroppings on the top of Old Rag and other mountains in the Blue Ridge are composed of granite that is more than a billion years old.

they are covering over the scars of cattle grazing, farming, and logging. Native animals are returning as well; black bears, raccoons, and opossums, America's only marsupials, now roam here again, as they did in pioneer days.

The park is bisected by the Skyline Drive, which runs along the crest of the mountains for approximately 105 miles. The roadway offers 75 overlooks and magnificent vistas of forests, mountains, and the historic Shenandoah Valley.

EXPLORING THE HISTORIC SHENANDOAH

Visitors to Shenandoah National Park can walk into the past by visiting the Corbin Cabin, a typical mountaineer's home. The cabin was built in 1910 by George Corbin and several of his friends, who cut and hewed its logs.

The Corbin family lived there for many years, subsisting on what they could grow or make. Today, the cabin is maintained by the Potomac Appalachian Trail Club, which rents it to members and the general public. The club also operates other rustic cabins along the Appalachian Trail.

At the Byrd Visitor Center, exhibits tell more of the story of the people who lived in these mountains from prehistoric times to the opening of the park. The park is also the home of Camp Hoover, which was President Hoover's getaway from Washington, D.C. Hoover's initial mandate for his retreat was fairly simple; he required it to be within 100 miles of the capital, at an elevation too high for mosquitos, and very close to a trout stream. Government officials still use the cabins at Camp Hoover on weekends.

Right: Thomas Jefferson, whose home in nearby Charlottesville looks out toward the Blue Ridge, much admired Dark Hallow Falls, a 70-foot cascade that flows through a rocky hollow near Big Meadows.

Left: During the fall, color dazzles the eyes at every turn in the road along lovely Skyline Drive.

SHENANDOAH NATIONAL PARK

Established: 1935

Location: Virginia

When to go: Open all year

Size: 196,466 acres

Terrain: Forested mountain ridge and valleys

Highlight: Corbin Cabin and Hogback Overlook

Wildlife: Bears, raccoons, deer, opossums, falcons, and birds

Activities: Ranger-led nature walks; auto tours, fishing, horseback riding, bicycling, hiking, cross-country skiing, and backpacking

Services: Two visitor centers, three park lodges, and five campgrounds

Information: Shenandoah National Park,
Box 348,
Luray, Virginia 22835;
703-999-2243

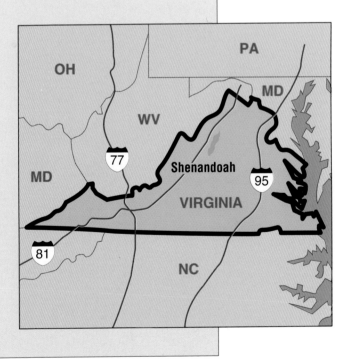

THEODORE ROOSEVELT

Where the West Begins

Theodore Roosevelt first arrived in Dakota Territory in 1883, just a few years after the end of the war between the Dakota tribe, or the Sioux, as they are better known, and the U.S. government.

Roosevelt came to bag a buffalo, but he ended up trying his hand at running cattle in the last years of open-range ranching. Soon after his arrival, the buffalo became virtually extinct, and unusually severe winters in 1886 and 1887 brought the cattle boom to a close. Roosevelt emerged from his experiences in the West a changed man; he had become a dedicated conservationist who went on to do more for our national park system than just about any politician before or since.

Theodore Roosevelt National Park is a surprisingly rugged landscape that stretches along North Dakota's Little Missouri River. Here, even a casual visitor can't help but feel a haunting sense of the Old West.

This austere landscape of rolling prairie cut by rivers and streams provides a habitat for an astonishing array of wildlife. Along with buffalo, elk, white-tailed and mule deer, and pronghorn antelope, there are wild horses and mountain lions, as well as millions of prairie dogs and other small mammals, reptiles, and amphibians. The theme song of the park seems to be the call of

the western meadowlark; it is a bright, flutelike sound that is unmistakable.

Today, the park includes significant portions of the Little Missouri Badlands, along with an important grassland area brimming with animal life and sections of the ranch property that once belonged to T.R. In the spring, when it is rainy, a spectacular bouquet made up of multitudes of wildflowers colors the river's bottomland and the grassy flats.

This is an uncrowded land, far removed from large urban centers. It is a place where visitors can experience the West and get used to lovely solitude in much the same way that young Teddy Roosevelt must have more than a century ago. The prairie dog towns still bustle, eagles

Above: The rustic cabin that served as the headquarters of Roosevelt's Maltese Cross Ranch is now being used as a visitor center.

Left: The parkland today looks much as it did when Teddy Roosevelt lived here in the 1880s. Now as then, the landscape has the "curious, fantastic beauty" that T.R. so enjoyed.

soar proudly through the sky, and stunning, seemingly endless sunsets brighten the evening sky. Little has changed.

The park is divided into two units about 60 miles apart. The park headquarters is in the town of Medora in the South Unit. Rich in the history and lore of the frontier, Medora was founded by a French nobleman and former cavalry officer, the Marquis de Mores, who named the town after his American wife, the daughter of a wealthy New York banker. The couple's 27-room prairie chateau broods over Medora from a bluff across the river—silent testimony to a place and age rapidly receding into the depths of time.

In sharp contrast to this grand house, the visitor center is located in the rustic cabin that was once the headquarters for T.R.'s cattle operation, the Maltese Cross Ranch. The cabin has been moved from its original site seven miles south. Roosevelt lived in the cabin in 1884 and 1885. From the Medora Overlook above town, visitors view the town as it might have appeared in Roosevelt's day.

If the South Unit is more historic, the North Unit may be more scenic and wild. Smaller and less closely associated with Roosevelt, the North Unit contains most of the park's wilderness. This part of the park gives visitors the feeling that they have entered an earlier era.

Here, the Little Missouri winds its spectacular course through rugged badlands where the cliffs seem higher, the canyons deeper, and the colored striations on the eroded rock more pronounced than elsewhere in this vast prairie wilderness. Oxbow Overlook provides a fine view of the Little Missouri River; it is a stunning vista with the blue river cutting through extensive badlands on either side.

Longhorn steers were brought to the park to commemorate the countless thousands of longhorns that were driven from Texas to the nearby Long-X ranch more than a century ago. They graze on the sagebrush flats in this place where the Old West still seems very much alive.

Opposite: Layers of rock and sediment form bands of color, known as striations, on the dome-shaped hills of the park.

Right: The Little Missouri River and its tributaries have been carving North Dakota's badlands—which Theodore Roosevelt once described as "a chaos of peaks, plateaus, and ridges"—for millions of years.

T.R. IN NORTH DAKOTA

Theodore Roosevelt once said that he would not have been president had it not been for his experiences in North Dakota.

In the fall of 1883, when he first came to the area shortly after the deaths of his mother and his first wife, Roosevelt purchased a small herd of cattle to run on the Maltese Cross Ranch. The next year he bought the rights to another ranch 30 miles away. He called it "Elkhorn" and always thought of it as his true home in North Dakota, while the Maltese Cross remained the center of his cattle business.

During 1885 and 1886, his ranching operations were quite successful, but during the bad winter the next year he lost 60 percent of his herd. At about the same time, the town of Medora began to decline. Roosevelt, newly married and involved in politics, gradually withdrew from the cattle business. The buildings at the Elkhorn Ranch have long since disappeared, but markers indicate where the ranch house stood. Few places yield a greater sense of Roosevelt during his western years.

The impact of Roosevelt's North Dakota experiences was powerful. As president, he established three national parks, helped found the U.S. Forest Service, and set aside millions of acres as national monuments.

Above: Despite their harsh appearance, the North Dakota Badlands support a great diversity of prairie animals, such as this mule deer doe and her fawns. Other commonly sighted animals include bison, pronghorns, prairie dogs, and wild horses.

Opposite: The badlands above the Little Missouri River; sediments erode beneath a much harder caprock, creating a flat-topped formation known as a rain pillar.

GEOLOGY OF THE CONTINENT'S CENTER

The history of North Dakota's badlands and prairie goes back at least 65 million years. As the Rocky Mountains rose up over the Great Plains, streams began to erode the peaks, carrying their sediment eastward and spreading mountain debris over the plains. Later, between five and 10 million years ago, the entire great plains were lifted up, and the Little Missouri River began to carve its badlands. The river's many small tributaries reshaped nearby areas.

The result of this continuous process of erosion by water is spectacular. There are wildly corrugated cliffs, twisted gullies, and rugged pinnacles. Dome-shaped hills, with layers of rock and sediment forming colored horizontal striations, run for miles and miles.

This wild region is the same today as when Theodore Roosevelt described the place as "a chaos of peaks, plateaus, and ridges."

THEODORE ROOSEVELT NATIONAL PARK

Established: 1978

Location: North Dakota

When to go: Open all year (winter access is limited)

Size: 70,446 acres

Terrain: Grassland prairie and badlands

Highlights: Elkhorn Ranch and Roosevelt's cabin

Wildlife: Buffalo, deer, elk, pronghorn antelopes, wild horses, mountain lions, prairie dogs, meadowlarks, small mammals, and snakes

Activities: Ranger-led walks, talks, tours of T.R.'s Maltese Cross cabin, and evening campfire programs; hiking, horseback riding, auto tours, canoeing, float trips, fishing, cross-country skiing, snowmobiling, and backpacking

Services: Three visitor centers and two campgrounds

Information: Theodore Roosevelt National Park, P.O. Box 7, Medora, North Dakota 58645; 701-623-4466

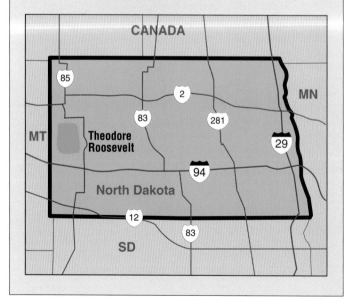

VIRGIN ISLANDS

Caribbean Paradise

Virgin Islands National Park, a unique national treasure in a beautiful setting, is one of just two national parks that do not lie within the 50 United States. (The other is located in American Samoa.)

Trunk Bay, on the northern side of St. John, offers one of the loveliest vistas in the entire Caribbean, a tropical region known for its exceptionally lovely views of lush isles, white beaches, towering mountains, and old pirate strongholds. The view from the bay is a series of beautiful, palm-ringed beaches glistening in the sun.

Sailboats dance in the sparkling blue water, and off in the distance, Whistling Cay, a small speck of land floating in an azure sea, seems to change color on the whim of the sky. During the nineteenth century, customs officers used the tiny island as a lookout for smugglers sailing between St. John and the nearby British Virgin Islands.

Within the park's borders are some 9,000 acres of spectacular Caribbean beaches, forests, and mountains, as well as 5,650 undersea acres and several stunning underwater nature trails. The park encompasses approximately three-quarters of St. John, the third largest of the U.S. Virgin Islands. Here you will find an incredible diversity of plant life, owing to a huge amount

of annual rainfall, as well as the island's exposure to spore-bearing winds. As you wander through high-elevation subtropical forests in the park's interior, you can see more than 800 plant species. At lower elevations, you can walk through dry, desertlike areas, as well as mangrove swamps that are rich with mangoes, palms, soursops, turpentine trees, and century plants.

St. John is one of about 100 jewellike islands that dot the blue waters of the northern Caribbean. The islands were visited by Colum-

Left: Moving like huge underwater clouds, swirling schools of fish are part of the exquisite world of form and color found beneath the surface of lovely Jumbia Bay.

Far Left: Built up over hundreds of thousands of years by tiny calcium-producing polyps, coral reefs attract a stunning variety of sea life just off St. John's beaches.

bus in 1493. Imagining the array of islands to be more extensive than it is, he named them for the 11,000 virgins who accompanied St. Ursula on her ill-fated pilgrimage to Rome.

For the next two centuries, the only Europeans to come to the islands were pirates, but in the seventeenth century, Danish settlers built vast sugar plantations using slave laborers imported from Africa. The Old World architecture of its towns and villages, coupled with its tropical climate and cooling trade winds, make the islands an ideal vacation spot.

The Virgin Islands owe their natural beauty to the fire of volcanoes. Geologists believe eruptions first occurred some 100 million years ago on the floor of the ocean. Over many eons, molten rock flowed from volcanic vents, forming the foundation of the island that we now know as St. John. About 30 million years after the island building began, the sea floor itself began to rise, lifted up by cataclysmic geologic forces.

The final phase in the construction of St. John was a series of violent eruptions above the sea that created a large island of solidified lava covered by sedimentary rocks, primarily limestone formed from the remains and secretions of marine plants and animals.

It was not long until seeds of plants borne aloft by the trade winds began the spectacular greening of St. John, preparing the island as a welcoming habitat for animals arriving from the mainland. The island's scores of bird species flew in of their own accord, but lizards and other reptiles no doubt floated ashore by accident.

UNDERWATER NATURE TRAIL

One of the most intriguing aspects of Virgin Islands National Park is its spectacular underwater realm. The park contains a stunning marine preserve where visitors can explore the complexity of life beneath the sea. Here are coral reefs, broad expanses of underwater grassland, and white sands moving slowly in the water. This lovely, complex, and extremely fragile community of plants and animals forms an exquisite and dynamic underwater reef ecosystem.

One of the park's nature trails lies beneath the sea in lovely Trunk Bay. Special underwater plaques guide snorkelers through the intricacies of the coral reefs. As you swim along the ten-foot-deep, 225-yard-long trail, signs explain how the reef was formed and indicate the kinds of underwater life you are likely to see. In addition to coral, you can observe brilliantly colored conchs, black sea urchins, brittle starfish, and other fascinating creatures.

Right: A scuba diver keeps an eye on a prowling shark. Coral reefs are a rich but exceedingly fragile environment, easily damaged by careless divers and boaters.

Opposite: A crescent of brilliant white sand is bordered by deep-green tropical forest and the turquoise waters of Hawksnest Bay, an excellent spot for snorkeling.

VIRGIN ISLANDS NATIONAL PARK

Established: 1956

Location: U.S. Virgin Islands

When to go: Open all year

Size: 14,689 acres

Terrain: Volcanic island ringed by beaches and coral reefs

Highlight: Trunk Bay

Wildlife: Brain coral, star coral, staghorn coral, coral shrimp, moray eels, and hundreds of species of fish, birds, and reptiles

Activities: Ranger-led hikes, snorkel tours, and interpretive talks; self-guided nature and underwater trails; snorkeling, swimming, boating, and fishing

Services: Visitor center, contact center, one campground, tent cottages, and new apartmentlike dwellings

Information: Virgin Islands National Park,
6310 Estate Nazareth,
St. Thomas, VI 00802 or
Box 7789,
Charlotte Amalie, St. Thomas, VI 00801;
809-775-6238

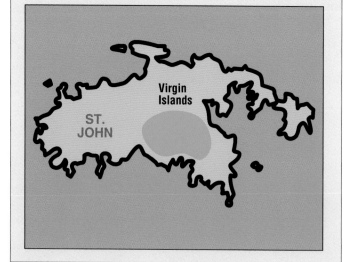

Right: Trunk Bay, seen here with Trunk and Whistling cays and Mary Point in the distance, is regarded by many travelers as one of the most beautiful beaches in the Caribbean.

VOYAGEURS

Northern Lakes

Canoeing on a lake in Voyageurs National Park, along the border of Minnesota and Canada, you are likely to hear the haunting cry of a loon echoing across the water. A bald eagle may fly in circles high overhead. At night, the eerie howls of wolves resound through the forest.

Throughout this great wilderness, blue herons stride confidently on their long legs, and mallards swim in and out among the grasses near the lakeshore. Great ospreys soar through the sky, their sharp eyes scanning the water for fish. Voyageurs encompasses a land of large lakes, with their shorelines cut by bays and inlets too numerous to count, as well as hundreds of small lakes, ponds, swamps, and one of the last remnants of the great wilderness forest that once blanketed this region.

Except for a brief gold rush in the area of Rainy Lake at the end of the nineteenth century, which left behind a mine shaft and tailings on Bushyhead Island, Voyageurs has always been wilderness. Most people who come here travel by canoe.

First the Sioux and then the Chippewa paddled through the wetlands to fish, hunt, gather cranberries, and harvest wild rice. Later, during the eighteenth and nineteenth centuries, French-Canadian voyageurs traveled through

the region in large canoes piled high with furs and trade goods. The voyageurs followed a route between northwest Canada and Montreal, often paddling their birch-bark canoes 16 or more hours a day.

Portaging, the carrying of canoes and gear to get around water that was not navigable, was the most difficult part of their lives. The annual trading route of the voyageurs included 120 separate portages. The most arduous was a nine-mile haul over hills and through swamps; appropriately it was called Grand Portage. The route of the voyageurs, celebrated by the park's miles of waterways and portages, became so important that it was used to define the border between the United States and British-held ter-

Above: Dressed in the style of a typical voyageur, a historical interpreter paddles his birchbark canoe along one of the park's waterways.

Left: Thousands of tiny islands dot the glassy surface of Rainy and Kabetogama lakes, offering refuge to a vast array of northern wildlife.

Above: Beavers are master architects and builders that carefully construct their dams and lodges using ax-sharp incisors and agile forepaws.

Right: Some 30 gray wolves (*Canis lupus*) range through Voyageurs National Park. Although sightings are rare, their distant howls are a familiar sound here.

Opposite: The waters of Rainy Lake, about 60 miles long and 12 miles wide, attract a variety of North Woods wildlife, including moose, beavers, black bears, and loons.

ritories in the treaty that put an end to the American Revolutionary War.

More than 35 percent of Voyageurs National Park is covered by water, most of it contained in four large lakes linked by narrow channels and small streams. There are many smaller lakes, as well as marshy areas and bogs. Visitors traveling through the park by canoe, motorboat, or houseboat often slip easily back and forth between the United States and Canada without knowing it.

A TRIP TO LOCATOR LAKE

Visitors can get to know some of the natural delights of Voyageurs National Park by taking a ranger-led trip from the Kabetogama Lake Visitor Center to Locator Lake.

The weekly trip includes travel by boat, canoe, and on foot. A boat takes visitors across Kabetogama Lake to a dock near La Bontys Point. From there you walk on a two-mile trail through a spruce bog and past a fascinating beaver dam and lodge. After you climb the ridge, the trail drops down through pine trees to the shore of Locator Lake.

The Park Service keeps several canoes cached at the site. With a ranger in the lead, visitors board canoes and paddle around the lovely woodland lake. The reward for this effort is the chance to see bald eagles, loons, ospreys, blue-winged teal, and, occasionally, herons.

Right: Sunrise lights up the sky over Namakan Lake, set on a vast expanse of wilderness between Voyageurs National Park and the Boundary Waters Canoe Area in Ontario.

Opposite: Autumn colors highlight maple and birch trees. Logging continued in the region until the early 1970s. Except on a few remote islands, the park is now covered with second- and third-growth forest.

VOYAGEURS NATIONAL PARK

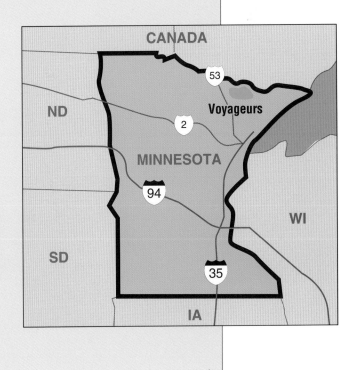

Established: 1975

Location: Minnesota

When to go: Open all year (winter access is limited)

Size: 218,036 acres

Terrain: Lakes, swamps, and forest

Highlight: Locator Lake

Wildlife: Bald eagles, ospreys, loons, beavers, herons, and wolves

Activities: Ranger-led walks and canoe trips; canoeing, boating, camping, hiking, fishing, swimming, water-skiing, snowmobiling, cross-country skiing, snowshoeing, and ice fishing

Services: Three visitor centers, park lodge, two hotels, and backcountry boat-in campsites

Information: Voyageurs National Park,
3131 Highway 53,
International Falls, Minnesota 56649;
218-283-9821

WIND CAVE

Caverns of Limestone

Buffalo, pronghorn antelope, and mule deer still roam the grassy hills of the Great Plains in South Dakota. Overhead, prairie falcons circle, looking for prey. To the northwest, the eastern flank of the pine-covered Black Hills looms in the distance.

But this tranquil world of prairie grass and sunshine is somewhat deceptive. Below the vast prairie, there is a great underground wonderland, where nature is putting on a spectacular display of geological artisanship.

Wind Cave is one of the largest caverns in the world, a labyrinth of passages carved out of limestone beds that have existed for 60 million years. Unlike many limestone caverns, including Mammoth Cave, that formed at relatively shallow depths—sometimes less than 100 feet—Wind Cave twists and turns its way through rock hundreds of feet below the surface. In one place the cavern is more than 600 feet below the surface.

The cave gets its name from the strong air currents that blow alternately in and out of the caverns. The direction of the wind depends on whether the air pressure in the cave is higher or lower than the atmospheric pressure outside. In a very real sense, the cave is breathing, and this constant rush of air, first in and then out, keeps the interior of the great cavern drier than most other caves. In Wind Cave, you won't hear the eerie sound of endlessly dripping and seeping water.

Because Wind Cave is not as wet as many other caves, there are almost no stalactites and stalagmites. Nature has worked a different kind of underground magic here. Instead of flowing through wide openings and depositing minerals in thick columns, water from the surface seeps through tiny cracks and

pores in the limestone. This seepage deposited a thin film, along with tiny droplets, on the walls and ceilings, creating a unique geological spectacle. Stunning multicolored encrustations decorate the walls and ceilings throughout the cavern.

Descriptive names explain the character of these startling works of nature. One kind of formation is called popcorn, a knobby growth that looks like splotches of coral of every size and shape. Another is called frostwork; it varies in size from small strands to large round formations that resemble snowballs. Wind Cave is probably most famous for what is undoubtedly the world's finest display of boxwork, a calcite formation resembling honeycomb. Boxwork is found everywhere in the cave, but the best examples are in the subterranean chambers called the Post Office, the Temple, and the Pearly Gates.

In 1881, brothers Jesse and Tom Bingham discovered this unique underground realm of wonders. Tom was chasing a

Above: Two worlds are preserved at Wind Cave National Park. On the surface, its 28,292 acres are a sanctuary of rolling grasslands and ponderosa forest. Below ground is a hidden world of dark and silent passages.

Opposite: At one time, 60 million buffalo spread out across the vast open land of the American West; now, small protected herds, like this one, bespeak the magnificence of those vanished multitudes.

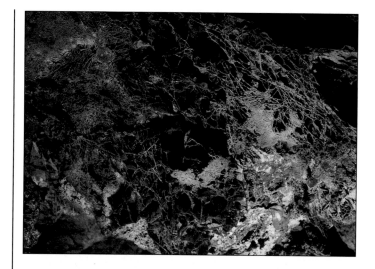

wounded antelope in a ravine when he heard a loud whistling noise. As he looked down, his hat was blown off his head by a powerful wind blowing directly out of a crack in the rocks. The brothers brought people to see the cave's wonders, and everyone who saw it seemed to want to develop it for a profit.

Several groups, one of them calling itself the Wonderful Wind Cave Improvement Company, competed for the right to mine the cave and lead tourists through it. In 1903, the federal government ended years of fierce bickering by establishing Wind Cave as a national park. It was the first cavern to be brought into the park system.

Top: The lacy boxwork in Wind Cave was created when water carrying dissolved crystals of calcium carbonate seeped through a network of cracks.

Bottom: The cave is decorated with a variety of unusual formations, such as this delicate aragonite "bush," created by the gradual accumulation of minerals.

FORMATION OF WIND CAVE

Roughly 335 million years ago, a shallow sea covered South Dakota. At that time North America was located on the earth's equator, and its climate was tropical. Gradually, the sea's water level dropped as the land rose and moved north. A layer of sediment grew to a thickness of between 300 and 600 feet.

About 320 million years ago, another sea inundated this area, depositing another layer of sediment several hundred feet thick on top of the first one. The forces that lifted the Black Hills created cracks in these limestone layers. Over a time span of millions of years, water seeped into these cracks, gradually dissolving the rock and creating the labyrinth of passages and chambers that we see now.

An unusual ecosystem also extends across the land above the cave. This area marks the boundary between the prairie and the ponderosa pine forests of the Black Hills. The grassland here is inhabited by prairie birds, such as falcons and meadowlarks, as well as nuthatches and wild turkeys that come from the forests.

WIND CAVE NATIONAL PARK

Established: 1903

Location: South Dakota

When to go: Open all year

Size: 28,295 acres

Terrain: Grassland prairie and underground caverns

Highlights: The Post Office and boxwork throughout the cave

Wildlife: Buffalo, pronghorn antelope, elk, deer, prairie dogs, falcons, meadowlarks, wild turkeys, and nuthatches

Activities: Ranger-led cave tours and campfire talks; scenic drives, nature trails, hiking, bicycling, and backpacking

Services: Visitor center, exhibits, and one campground

Information: Wind Cave National Park, R.R. 1, Box 190, Hot Springs, South Dakota 57747; 605-745-4600

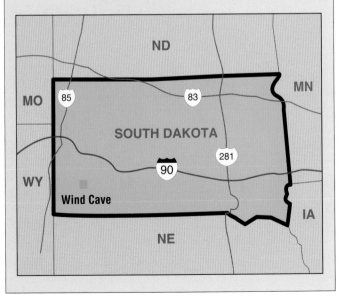

Top: Helictite "bushes" form on a cave wall. With more than 75 miles of explored passages, Wind Cave is the third longest cave in the United States and one of the most complex underground chambers in the world.

Bottom: Prairie dogs are highly social animals, living in colonies or "towns" made up of dozens of burrows with interconnecting tunnels. They can often be seen standing on their burrow mounds, keeping an eye out for intruders.

WRANGELL-ST. ELIAS

Awesome Wilderness

Wrangell-St. Elias National Park in Alaska stands out for the sheer audacity of its topography—no small claim in a land where mountains and glaciers go on for hundreds of miles at a stretch.

Three great mountain ranges converge in the park, creating a reckless jumble of ragged peaks, lovely river valleys, and enormous glaciers. The St. Elias Mountains, the world's tallest coastal range, shove their way up from the Yukon Territory in the southeast, where in a torrent of glaciers and ice fields they join the Chugach Range. The mighty Wrangell Range, coming down from the north, is the backbone of the park.

Near the point where the three ranges come together, in the southeast corner of the park, spectacular Mount St. Elias rises 18,008 feet. It is the second tallest mountain in the United States (Denali, otherwise known as Mount McKinley, is the tallest). Only 30 miles from the rugged, glacier-scoured coast of the Gulf of Alaska, Mount St. Elias rises so dramatically and precipitously that it dominates its surroundings like few other mountains.

Elsewhere in the park are eight more of the 16 tallest peaks in the United States; four of them are above 16,000 feet. As you fly over the park, the mountains come at you in waves of ranges that change color with the weather.

Floating on a raft down one of the park's many rivers, you will see Dall sheep on the tundra and mountain goats on the rocky crags of mountain slopes. But there are so many huge glaciers in this park that there is not very much habitable terrain. The park's largest glacier, Malaspina, is so big that Rhode Island could fit on it.

This rugged region has been called the Himalayas of North America. In fact, the rugged terrain of the park may actually be wilder than the great Asian mountains. There are still valleys in these mighty Alaskan mountains where people probably have never set foot, and countless peaks remain unnamed and unscaled. The park is so vast that it contains more unexplored terrain than the Himalayas, largely as a result of the short summers and long winters that come with its proximity to the Arctic.

The park's size is overwhelming: The biggest national park by far, it is larger than Switzerland and six times the size of Yellowstone. But it is not inaccessible. Two roads lead into the heart of the park. The road from the Chitina River Valley goes to two tiny towns that are remnants of the gold and copper mining frenzy at the turn of the century. Today, these communities are staging areas for hiking, rafting, climbing, and kayaking adventures in the park.

Left: A breaching whale in the frigid waters off the park's southern coast. Marine mammals, including harbor seals and several species of whales, are often seen around Malaspina Glacier and Icy Bay.

Opposite: Encased in ice and snow, Mount St. Elias rises 18,000 feet over the surface of Icy Bay. The Saint Elias Mountains spill over into Canada's Kluane Park, which, together with Wrangell-St. Elias, has been named a United Nations World Heritage Site.

Tyndall Glacier flows
below jagged
mountain peaks. At
least 150 glaciers
slowly grind away at
the park's three
mountain ranges.

Right: Measuring
more than 13 million
acres, Wrangell-St.
Elias is the largest
national park,
providing wild
animals like this black
bear plenty of room
to roam.

Opposite: The
peaks of the
Wrangell Mountains
as seen from the
Chitina-McCarthy
Road, one of only
two roadways that
lead into the park.

VISITING ALASKA'S PAST

One of Wrangell-St. Elias's two good unpaved roads leads visitors back in time to the Alaska gold rush days at the turn of the century.

From the ranger station at Chitina on the east side of the park, the road follows the abandoned Copper River and Northwest Railroad for 62 miles to its end. There, a hand-pulled cable tram takes you across the Kennicott River to the tiny community of McCarthy. Now almost deserted, it was once a town of 2,000 miners, hustlers, and card sharks.

From the McCarthy side of the river, where you can rent a bicycle or hire a taxi, another dirt road leads to the ghost town of Kennicott, the site of a 13-story mill that was abandoned in 1938. The mill and other deserted buildings here are covered with ferrous-oxide red paint and trimmed in white. They are among Alaska's finest and most photogenic samples of turn-of-the-century structures.

The copper mine at Kennicott, now on the National Register of Historic Places, was once the world's richest.

WRANGELL-ST. ELIAS NATIONAL PARK

Established: 1980

Location: Alaska

When to go: Summer

Size: 13,188,335 acres

Terrain: Mountains, glaciers, and valleys

Highlight: Kennicott town site

Wildlife: Dall sheep, mountain goats, bears, wolves, moose, boreal owls, ospreys, salmon, small mammals, and birds

Activities: Horseback riding, pack trips, river running, kayaking, lake fishing, mountain climbing, hiking, aerial sightseeing, and backpacking

Services: Visitor center, three ranger and information stations outside park boundaries, two private campgrounds, three lodges, and one bed-and-breakfast

Information: Wrangell-St. Elias National Park,
P.O. Box 29,
Glennallen, Alaska 99588;
907-822-5234

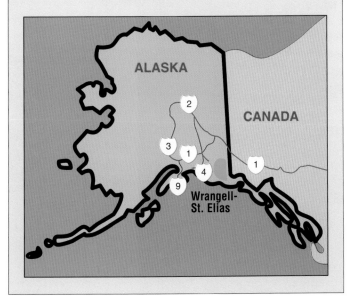

YELLOWSTONE

Thermal Wonderland

The volcanic cauldron beneath Yellowstone National Park creates enormous plumes of water belching out of the earth from steaming vents. More than half of the world's 20,000 geysers are located within the park, and the area is also blessed with a proliferation of hot springs, fumaroles, and teaming pools of evanescent colors and algae.

Here one encounters percolating streams, bubbling creeks, and gushing rivers, and almost everywhere in the park, the acrid and unmistakable smell of sulfur.

In 1872, when Yellowstone was made the world's first national park, Wyoming was not yet a state, and the United States was still a pioneer nation. Its western frontiers overflowed with splendid scenery and a profusion of wild animals. Small wonder, then, that the first visitors to the park did not come to see wilderness. Yellowstone was attractive to them because of its extraordinary wealth of geysers and fumaroles. These hearty adventurers made the arduous trek to the remote park by rail and by wagon.

In the intervening century, civilization moved west, and the frontier, including most of the animals, disappeared. The thermal extravaganza is still as spectacular as ever. But today's visitors to Yellowstone also appreciate the park as a

sanctuary for wildlife and a preserve of pristine wilderness.

Yellowstone's boundaries encompass some of America's most spectacular untouched wilderness: jagged peaks, endless forests, rugged canyons, crystal-clear lakes, and alpine meadows. Roaming this terrain is an array of western wildlife unmatched elsewhere: buffalo, elk, deer, grizzly bears, black bears, ospreys, eagles, coyotes, cougars, beavers, white pelicans, and moose. More than two million acres of Rocky Mountain wilderness provide a safe and vast habitat for all this wildlife.

Nature runs by its own time schedule in Yellowstone. This is a place to sit still and let the

Above: The park has five entrances, and all can get crowded in the summer. Roads are open from early May through October, depending on local weather conditions.

Left: Part of Lake Yellowstone, which covers more than 100 square miles, laps at the base of the rugged Absaroka Range.

magic of nature amaze you. It won't be long before the show begins. You may catch the colors of a rainbow through a plummeting waterfall. Hike along a marsh, and in time you might see a bull moose stride out of the forest and wade through ankle-deep water. Or you may see a family of black bears romping and wrestling in a meadow beside a mountain stream. Keep your eyes on the high branches of a lodgepole pine long enough, and eventually the head of a bald eagle may emerge from the thicket of its nest.

Stand quietly on a bank of the Yellowstone River; a merganser paddles along enjoying the day. Upstream, a cutthroat trout leaps out of the water to see what the duck is doing, but the fish is oblivious to the danger of the great osprey cir-

cling 200 feet overhead. Watch closely, because the bird is incredibly swift when it dives for its prey.

Early in the morning during the autumn, you may hear the eerie bugling of a bull elk, but then again you may not. Even the park's thermal attractions operate on their own secret timetables: Old Faithful erupts every 50 to 80 minutes, not on the hour as many of us learned in school.

An enduring myth about Yellowstone holds that Native Americans stayed away from the area because of its strange and frightening thermal features. In fact, people have lived here since the retreat of the most recent ice age nearly 9,000 years ago. In 1807, a Native American probably told trapper John Colter about a place where hot water and steam issue

Right: A bison crosses the Firehole River near Old Faithful. The steaming river is heated in three geyser basins before flowing into the Madison River.

Left: Splashing down from a height of more than 300 feet, the Lower Falls propels the raging river through Yellowstone's Grand Canyon between rugged walls of volcanic rock dyed brilliant yellow by minerals in the water.

from the earth. This member of the Lewis and Clark expedition is credited with the "discovery" of Yellowstone.

Then as now, it was obvious that this is an extraordinary place where something highly unusual is going on beneath the surface of the earth to create this garden of thermal wonders. Geologists discovered that the earth's crust is extraordinarily thin in the Yellowstone region. In most places on the planet, the crust is about 20 miles thick and floats on a mantle that consists of molten rock, or magma. In Yellowstone, the earth's crust is only about two miles thick. The seething

GEYSERS AND FUMAROLES

Geysers, springs of hot bubbling water, or fumaroles issuing sulfurous steam seem to occur almost everywhere you turn in Yellowstone. Elsewhere there are mud pots and underground explosions, or the earth is hot to the touch. Obviously, something spectacular is going on just below the surface.

To understand the thermal wonders in Yellowstone today, we need to go back 75 million years to a time when sections of the earth's crust collided and raised the Rocky Mountains to far greater heights than we now see. About 25 million years later, volcanic activity created still more mountain ranges in the Yellowstone region.

The grand finale of this geological activity occurred about 600,000 years ago, when an area within the boundaries of the park suddenly exploded as two giant magma chambers moved to within a few thousand feet of the earth's surface. The landscape was devastated, and volcanic ash and dust spread over thousands of square miles. At the center, only a smoldering caldera remained; this enormous, collapsed crater covered an area that was 47 by 27 miles.

Geologists believe that Yellowstone's boiling hot springs, mud holes, and geysers are reminders that more violent geological activity is destined to happen again.

Right: Mighty Old Faithful regularly sends majestic columns of water shooting as high as 200 feet into the Wyoming sky.

Opposite: At Mammoth Hot Springs, superheated water rises to the surface through limestone rather than lava, creating terraces of smooth travertine.

hot mantle heats the ground above it, which in turn heats the water in the springs and geysers.

Celebrated in anecdote, cartoon, and caricature, Yellowstone is the place most people probably think of when asked to name a national park. It is also a study of the way in which a park should be run, but this was not always the case. During Yellowstone's first decade as a national park, geysers were vandalized; game, particularly bison, was slaughtered by park officials and hunters; and politicians gave away its land as concessions to supporters.

In 1886, the U.S. Army took over administration of the park and built roads and the park headquarters near the north boundary. The park became a model of efficiency, which operators of other parks in the fledgling park system attempted to imitate. Beginning in 1916, when it was established, the National Park Service has administered the park with dedication and skill.

Bottom Right: Fireweed blossoms next to logs that were charred by the great fire of 1988. The fire swept across some 790,000 acres, more than a third of the park.

Below: Waterways throughout the park attract a variety of wildlife, including moose, beavers, black bears, and many species of waterfowl.

YELLOWSTONE WINTER

Many people who know and love Yellowstone believe that the park is at its best during the cold winter months, from December to March. The only road open runs across the northern tier of the park, from the north to the northeast entrance, providing access to the little town of Cooke City, Montana.

During these cold months, the park is more pristine than it is during the busy warm months. Rivers in deep valleys are covered by ice; snow-mantled mountains contrast brightly with clear blue skies; and wildlife, not people, predominate. The park is a fantasyland of snow, ice, and steam.

Lodging facilities within the park, although limited, are available. There are more than 50 miles of trails for cross-country skiers, and snowmobiling is permitted on many unplowed roads. There are also tours in heated snow coaches.

Left: Yellowstone is justly celebrated for its great trout fishing. Catch limits vary throughout the park, however, and a permit is required.

YELLOWSTONE NATIONAL PARK

Established: 1872

Location: Wyoming, Montana, and Idaho

When to go: Open all year (winter access is limited)

Size: 2,221,766 acres

Terrain: Mountains, canyons, lakes, geysers, and hot springs

Highlights: Old Faithful Geyser and Grand Canyon of the Yellowstone River

Wildlife: Elk, grizzly bears, black bears, deer, moose, eagles, ospreys, beavers, mountain lions, and trumpeter swans

Activities: Ranger-led walks, talks, and campfire programs; hiking, camping, fishing, boating, horseback riding, photography courses, bicycling, stagecoach rides, cross-country skiing, snowshoeing, snowmobiling, snowcoach tours, and backpacking

Services: Four visitor centers, eight lodges and cabins, and 13 campgrounds

Information: Yellowstone National Park, P.O. Box 168, Yellowstone National Park, Wyoming 82190; 307-344-7381

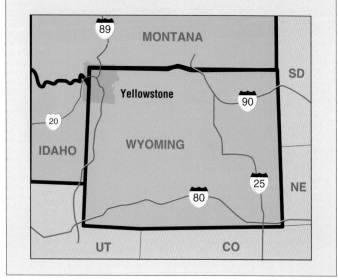

Right: Morning Glory Pool in Upper Geyser Basin brings to the surface a glorious spectrum of color from deep within the earth.

YOSEMITE

Sculpted by Ice

The spectacularly beautiful natural setting of Yosemite Valley inspired one of its early explorers to write, "As I looked at the grandeur of the scene, a peculiar exalted sensation seemed to fill my whole being, and I found my eyes in tears with emotion."

Visitors today find themselves equally moved by this profoundly lovely gorge, cut by the Merced River, with its sides gouged out by glaciers into enormous monoliths. Granite cliffs rise 3,000 feet above a forested floor, a tranquil and solemn river flows grandly through its proud channel, and waterfalls tumble from the heights. The famed Yosemite Falls is 2,425 feet high, which makes it North America's highest waterfall.

The grandeur of Yosemite tugs at the soul. A park ranger was once asked what he would do if he had only one day to visit Yosemite Valley. The ranger replied, "I'd weep." Whether apocryphal or not, the anecdote contains much truth about this grassy, tree-filled defile cut deep into the heart of the Sierra Nevada. Although it contains less than one half of one percent of the total area of the park, this valley is undoubtedly what most people think of when they think of Yosemite.

The gorge is guarded by two famous sentinel rocks; their massive shapes are well known

around the globe. The park's most famous landmark, Half Dome, with its great sheared-off face, rises 4,800 feet above the eastern end of the valley. El Capitan, a monolith that rises 3,600 feet above the evergreens along the Merced River, stands sentinel at the western entrance. One of the most precipitous cliffs in the world, El Capitan, which in Spanish means "the chief," is made of granite so hard and crack-free that the powerful forces of erosion scarcely seem to affect it.

Beyond this justifiably famous valley, the park is a showcase for the wonders of nature. This vast and varied domain includes giant sequoias, alpine meadows, peaks soaring above 13,000 feet, lovely alpine lakes, sparkling trout streams, grassy meadows, and glacial remnants. The range

Above: Hikers on the Mist Trail take in the thundering cascades of the Merced River as it tumbles over Vernal Falls into Yosemite Valley.

Opposite: Yosemite Falls leaps down a sheer rock face in a series of cascades that looks like a single mighty waterfall. At 2,425 feet, it is the highest waterfall in North America.

Right: The unmistakable granite mass of El Capitan, carved by a mantle of glacial ice as much as a mile thick, is mirrored in the icy Merced River.

Opposite: Contrary to appearances, there never was another half to Half Dome. The shape of the famous landmark is the result of exfoliation, a process by which rock sheds its outer layers along fault lines.

of natural features is so diverse because of Yosemite's location in the temperate climate of central California and an unusually varied terrain, ranging from desert to high alpine.

Within the park, there are four of the seven life zones found on the North American continent. At its lowest elevations, a desertlike environment harbors the brush rabbit and chaparral. Next are mid-elevation forests and the valley floors that provide a haven for mule deer and chipmunks. Moving up in altitude, the red fir and Jeffrey pine of high-elevation forests take over. This is where deer and the park's resident black bears migrate in spring. Higher still is a colder and harsher subalpine world. This land is dominated by rock, snow, and ice.

Where soil has been able to cover the rocky landscape, meadows appear, providing a habitat for such small animals as the marmot and pika. Dwarf willows and dozens of wildflower species dot the landscape. Tuolumne Meadows, one of the park's most cherished features, is a vast expanse of flowing grass, cut by the lovely Tuolumne River and circled by peaks of the Sierra. Millions of years ago, the meadow was under a vast sheet of ice nearly half a mile thick.

The park contains three groves of giant sequoias. These towering monuments of another age are second only to bristlecone pine trees in age among all living things. Each of the groves, which are widely separated by less lofty forests of pine and ponderosa, contains several hundred giant trees.

Yosemite: Sculpted by Ice

The best known of the three, Mariposa Grove, has about 200 sequoia trees, which rise so far above the thick, bouncy forest floor that you are only dimly aware of their tops. One of the oldest is called the Grizzly Giant. Believed to be the fifth largest tree in the world, Grizzly Giant is estimated to be 2,700 years old, with a weight of 1,000 tons; its top rises more than 200 feet above the ground.

Separated by about 35 miles, Mariposa Grove and Yosemite Valley played seminal roles in the history of America's national parks. Native Americans had known about the wonders of Yosemite Valley for centuries, but it was not discovered by white men until the mid-nineteenth century.

This startling piece of wilderness wonderland was probably first viewed from the rim as early as the 1830s, but the first white men to enter the valley were a pair of '49er miners who were tracking a wounded bear. In 1851, an Army bat-talion entered the valley in pursuit of Ahwahneechee warriors, and by 1855 the first tourist wagons were creaking through the valley over old Indian trails. Soon afterward, toll roads and hotels were opened by local entrepreneurs.

In 1864, President Abraham Lincoln signed a bill giving Mariposa Grove and Yosemite Valley to the state of California to protect it in perpetuity. This was the first time any nation had established a wilderness preserve within its own boundaries. Following the creation of Yellowstone National Park in 1872, early conservationists, particularly John Muir, urged that Yosemite also be established as a national park.

Yosemite National Park was finally mandated in 1890, but it was administered as two separate state parks for 16 more years. Thanks to the foresight of President Lincoln, John Muir, and others, it remains sublimely beautiful, an incomparable masterpiece of nature.

Right: The mountains and mighty trees of Yosemite, according to naturalist John Muir, are "open to the divine soul, dissolved in the mysterious, incomparable spirit of holy light."

Opposite: A true geological wonder, El Capitan, located at the west end of Yosemite Valley, is the largest single block of granite in the world.

CONSTRUCTION OF EL CAPITAN

Yosemite Valley was formed by glaciers during a Pleistocene ice age. At the beginning of the epoch, the terrain now occupied by the Sierra Nevada was covered with low ridges, hills, and valleys. An ancient predecessor of the Merced River flowed through this quiet landscape.

Over eons, a gradual upheaval powered by awesome geologic forces beneath the earth tilted the Sierra block. This caused the fledgling river to pick up speed and rush toward the sea. As its flow increased in velocity, the river began carving its way down through the bedrock. Eventually a 2,000-foot V-shaped valley was cut.

Millions of years later, the climate changed, and great ice sheets began spreading across the area and into the valley. Over time the glaciers ground the valley into a steep U-shaped defile, rounding peaks along its sides into great domes. Advancing and receding three times, the glaciers eventually melted, leaving a lake-covered valley. In time the lake disappeared.

The result of all this erosion is a flat-bottomed, forested valley floor with monumental monoliths rising above sheared canyon walls. The famous domed rock, El Capitan, is larger than the Rock of Gibraltar. Geologists believe it may be the largest single block of granite in the world. Its spectacular 3,000-foot face draws rock climbers from around the world.

From the valley floor, visitors often see the tiny figures of climbers making the daring ascent of the cliff. During the climb, which takes several days, they sleep in slings hanging from minuscule cracks or ledges in the cliff face.

PIONEER YOSEMITE HISTORY CENTER

Spectacular geology notwithstanding, Yosemite has a fascinating history to tell. At Wawona, near the south entrance, the Pioneer Yosemite History Center gives visitors a real sense of the past. Restored buildings have the look and feel of the nineteenth century. Visitors can chat with costumed guides who portray homesteaders, cavalry officers, farmers, and mountaineers.

One of the stories you are likely to hear at the history center relates the origin of the name Yosemite. According to the tale, when the Mariposa Battalion tracked an Ahwahneechee war party accused of raiding nearby mountain trading posts into the valley, the warriors yelled something that sounded like "Yo Shay Ma Tee" or "Yo Ha Mi Tee."

The expression, meaning "some of them are killers," was usually reserved for grizzly bears, not other people. Apparently thinking this was the Ahwahneechee Indian name for the area, the soldiers gave an approximation of it to the glorious valley.

Left: Sentinel Rock, one of the many dramatic granite formations that ring Yosemite Valley, stands more than 7,000 feet high.

Opposite Left: The Merced River plummets 317 feet over the sheer granite ledge of Vernal Falls. The short but steep Mist Trail leads to an overlook at the top of the falls.

Opposite Right: Dozens of creeks and streams feed the two major rivers, the Merced and Tuolomne, that wind through lush, high-country meadows before flowing out of the park.

YOSEMITE NATIONAL PARK

Established: 1890

Location: California

When to go: Open all year (winter access is limited)

Size: 761,170 acres

Terrain: Deep gorges, forests, mountains, and meadows

Highlights: El Capitan, Mariposa Grove, and Yosemite Falls

Wildlife: Mule deer, bears, squirrels, rabbits, marmots, pikas, and dozens of bird species

Activities: Ranger-led talks and walks, evening and children's programs, bike rides, and history tours; auto tape tours, bus and tram tours, stagecoach rides, films, plays, concerts, art and photography classes, music workshops, museum, horseback riding, climbing, fishing, rafting, swimming, boating, ice-skating, cross-country and downhill skiing, and backpacking

Services: Two visitor centers, history center, nature center, five lodges, cabins, and 15 campgrounds

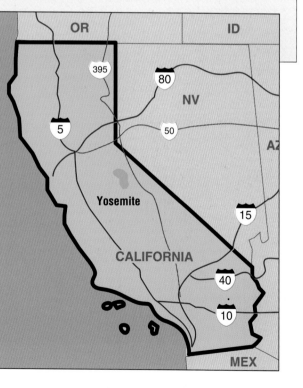

Right: Covered with patches of snow, the rocky face of Mammoth Peak is reflected in an alpine tarn near 9,945-foot Tioga Pass, the highest paved road in the Sierra Nevada.

ZION

Monumental Desert Valley

Elongated shadows cross the floor of Zion Canyon in the early morning, while sunlight bathes the tops of massive sandstone towers. Mormon settlers gave these natural wonders biblical names, such as the Altar of Sacrifice, the Court of the Patriarchs, and Angels Landing. But even without these appropriately reverential names, the great figures, hulking 2,000 feet above the canyon floor, command our respect and awe. This narrow, curving gorge seems to cut through time itself.

Zion is a canyon of spectacular and enormous scale. Its perpendicular cliffs are nearly 3,000 feet high. Its great rock figures are imposing and monolithic, as are the monumental buttresses, deep hanging canyons, rock landings, and alcoves that have been gouged out of the cliff faces. In contrast to this grandeur, the upper end of Zion Canyon, just a few miles away, is so narrow that two people standing side by side can touch both of the canyon's rock walls. The canyon is so deep that the sun penetrates to its floor for only minutes each day.

Unlike other canyon parks—including Canyonlands, Bryce, and the Grand Canyon, where many visitors view the canyons from their rims—Zion draws visitors to its floor. From that vantage point, they look up at the stupendous perpendicular topography. Walking along the Virgin River, which created this scenic spectacle, park visitors gain a unique perspective on nature.

As they contemplate the great rock figures towering above them from the serenity of groves of Fremont cottonwood, willow, and box elder trees, which line the canyon floor, visitors feel the unusual serenity of this unique place. Here, only muted sounds interrupt the special reverence the canyon in-

spires: the song of a quail, water trickling down a side valley, or the wind blowing through the leaves.

This great canyon in the desert has drawn human visitors since ancient times. Archaeological remnants indicate that people lived in the canyon as early as A.D. 500. They were probably wandering groups of weavers who hunted small game and gathered food in the area. Later, the Anasazi settled more permanently in the southern end of the canyon, where they built pueblos and irrigation systems to water their crops of corn and beans. The Anasazi disappeared from the area abruptly during the thirteenth century.

In the early-eighteenth century, Spanish priests and soldiers who were exploring the high plateau country north of the Grand Canyon, in what is now southwestern Utah, came upon the canyon. After the arrival of the Spanish explorers,

Left: Many of the park's fantastic scenic attractions are visible from the roadway, but more adventurous visitors have the option of venturing into the backcountry on foot—or on horseback.

Opposite: The park's scenic drive winds into a landscape carved by millenia of rain, flash floods, and steadily flowing rivers. Zion Canyon, for example, has cut a channel into the earth as deep as 3,000 feet .

Zion: Monumental Desert Valley

stories of the canyon's wonders began to spread. Later in the century, the famed trapper Jedediah Smith came south from his headquarters to determine the commercial possibilities of the canyon. In the middle of the nineteenth century, several families of Mormon pioneers began using the canyon as a place of special reverence, developing it as a religious retreat.

Zion Canyon was sculptured over the course of a million years by the flowing waters of the Virgin River sifting down through layer after layer of the red and white Navajo sandstone that forms the canyon's sheer walls. The layers of sedimentary sandstone and limestone had been a desert 15 million years ago. Gradually, these layers were pushed upwards

to form the 1,500-square-mile Markagunt Plateau. Then the Virgin River went to work carving out the monumental canyon. Drawn relentlessly by gravity, it slices its way through the rock down to the desert floor below.

ANGELS LANDING

Well-named Angels Landing is a rock pinnacle that rises 1,500 feet above the valley floor of Zion Canyon. Visitors reach its airy and dangerous summit by following the West Rim Trail, one of the most beautiful trails in the western United States.

The trail leads through a series of long switchbacks up the canyon wall to Refrigerator Canyon. Many people take a break in a glen of piñon pine and big-tooth maple before negotiating a series of steep switchbacks, called Walters Wiggles.

A sign points to what looks like a nearly impossible route atop a narrow ridge that leads to the summit of Angels Landing. The rock drops straight down on either side for more than 1,000 feet, but there are chains strung along the path and footholds cut into the rock to make the trail as safe as possible.

The vista from the summit is well worth the effort. It is one of the grandest sights anywhere: a 360-degree view of Zion Canyon. A huge rock monolith, called the Great White Throne, seems to be within a stone's throw in one direction, and there is a startling view of what now appears to be a tiny Virgin River meandering through minuscule trees far below.

ZION NATIONAL PARK

Established: 1919

Location: Utah

When to go: Open all year (the main season is March through October)

Size: 146,597 acres

Terrain: Deep canyon with its rim in high desert plateau

Highlights: Angels Landing and Checkerboard Mesa

Wildlife: Mountain lions, mule deer, ring-tailed cats, rattlesnakes, reptiles, and 270 species of birds

Activities: Ranger-led nature walks, talks, evening program, and children's program; hiking, horseback trail rides, tram tours, climbing, bicycling, river tubing, cross-country skiing, and backpacking (by permit)

Services: Two visitor centers, a park lodge, and three campgrounds

Information: Zion National Park, Springdale, Utah 84767; 801-772-3256

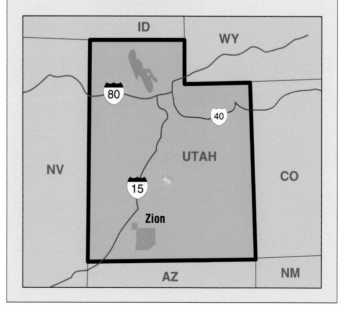

Opposite: Named by Mormon settlers, the Great White Throne is a massive sandstone monolith that rises almost 2,500 feet above the canyon floor.

INDEX